MATCH FISHING WITH
BENNY ASHURST

By the same author

FISHING THE NORFOLK BROADS

MATCH FISHING WITH

BENNY ASHURST

PETER COLLINS

ERNEST BENN LIMITED
LONDON & TONBRIDGE

Published by Ernest Benn Limited
25 New Street Square, London EC4A 3JA
& Sovereign Way, Tonbridge, Kent TN9 1RW
First impression 1968
Second impression 1975
© Peter Collins 1968
Printed in Great Britain
ISBN 0–510–21411–8

Contents

Illustrations

Drawings in Text

Foreword

THE NAME BENNY ASHURST needs no introduction. And there are few established match anglers who do not know the man himself. Now 52 years of age, Benny has been a match angler for thirty-three years and has won over 300 contests—a record that very few men indeed can equal.

Match fishing is his life. It is very rarely out of his thoughts and he is relentlessly dedicated to improving match angling techniques. Already he has made what is probably the biggest-ever contribution by an individual, his stick floats and caster style being widely used on flowing rivers. His peacock quill floats are also of the very highest quality and the bait that he produces on his Lancashire maggot farm is in wide demand throughout the country. There is none better.

Benny was a coal miner for twenty-five years but suffered a compound fractured thigh during an accident underground. During the eight months he was in hospital he planned his return to match fishing. He talked his way out of hospital and, encased in plaster around the chest, lower body and one leg, hobbled to the Fir Tree flash at Leigh and won a match virtually lying on his side.

And in 1951 he was involved in a car accident in which he suffered a fractured wrist, a broken leg below the knee and severe head injuries. He came round briefly after the collision and, trapped in the vehicle, was heard to say 'I shall never fish again'. But newspaper bills in the Leigh area 'Local angler killed in car crash' were premature. Benny's determination to live saw him through. Only two months later, with one arm in plaster, he was placed fourth out of 500 in the Bottislow open match with 4 lb. 11 oz. of tiny fish all caught one-handed. Stoke City AA president Alex Proffitt still tells the story of Benny's achievement that day, calling it the finest performance he has ever seen.

Benny has won a lot of money at match fishing but he has also been a teacher. His son Kevin is already widely acknowledged to be one of the best matchmen of his generation and much of the credit belongs to Benny. He will always find time to tell other anglers how he fishes but has an eager ear for anything progressive that can further improve the art of match fishing.

Benny Ashurst, a living legend, now tells the story of his lifetime in match fishing. It is rich in experience, an almost incredible tale of success, coupled with precise detail of the methods that brought him so many fish and such wide acclaim. No one man can climb all the peaks of angling ability and Benny makes no claim to be a specimen fish angler. That aspect of fishing never interested him. But there is no better matchman in this country.

It has been a very real pleasure to help him tell his story.

PETER COLLINS

1. My Road to Success

MY DEDICATED INTEREST in fishing didn't develop until I was nineteen years old. I had the same mild interest in fishing as any other young lad but I didn't take it seriously until I was nineteen. This sudden enthusiasm came when I married and moved from West Horton, a Lancashire village eight miles from Leigh. I moved to Leigh and lived in a house close to the edge of Fir Tree flash.

This flash—a still-water lake formed as the result of subsidence from colliery workings, and naturally filled with water—was full of roach and also held plenty of perch. I started to fish it when I moved to Leigh, fishing for the roach with bread bait. I didn't buy maggots since these couldn't then be bought in the area. Most of the anglers who used maggots bred their own at that time. Occasionally I was lucky and one of them would give me some maggots but bread fishing was the easy way out.

Bread was cheap and easy to obtain and it proved by results that it was a tip-top bait. But, while fishing myself, I also used to take a keen interest in other anglers, watching how they fished, the tackle they used, the bait they preferred and had a keen eye on anything affecting the catching of fish.

The local club was the Fir Tree Angling Club. This was a club of competent anglers. It wasn't easy to join. The fee was £2—expensive by standards of that era and to qualify for membership each man had to be a proficient angler. I spent hours watching members of this club fishing the flash and I was occasionally invited to fish in the sweepstake contests they sometimes held after one of their club matches.

I was still a bread angler first and foremost. And as the result of my wide experience of fishing the flash—where most of the matches were held—I even began to win one or two of these sweepstakes, even though I was not yet a member of the club.

The secretary of the Fir Tree club, Wilf Dyson, was very good to me. He realised I had an all-consuming interest in fishing and helped me with advice and sometimes with maggots when I wanted them.

The standard of skill of members was very high. Perhaps, as a youngster, it seemed higher to me then than it actually was, but I had

11

nothing but admiration for these men. They made their own rods, twelve foot Spanish reed rods that seemed as light as feathers. They also used three and a half inch wooden centre-pin reels which in those days cost about twelve shillings and sixpence each.

The top rod maker was Bob Clark. I badly wanted one of his rods which cost, even in those days, five pounds each. I couldn't afford that much money for a rod, having only recently married. But I did buy a second-hand rod for twenty-five shillings which I worked on and adapted for use in the flash. I improved the rings and lightened it as much as possible until it was at least a good if not an outstanding rod.

I suppose all this enthusiasm, not only in fishing every spare minute of the time I had to spare from coal-mining but also in acquiring the best possible tackle with limited resources, impressed the members of the Fir Tree Club.

My big moment came at one annual meeting. After the presentation of club prizes the committee discussed applications for membership—and Wilf Dyson put my name forward. I was twenty then, a youngster indeed, but part reason for the club's desire to make me a member was that I lived on the bank of the flash and they wanted me to sell their day tickets!

The day following the presentation there was to be a big match of the Leigh Association of Anglers. This was an annual event fished on the Leigh Canal. Wilf had already entered me for this match. But I wasn't very keen. I had never fished the canal, although it was little further from my home than the flash. I didn't fancy it. It had never impressed me as a fishery. I had watched anglers fishing there but I had never seen them catch many fish. I had thought this was hardly the place to learn to fish since experience and knowledge only come by catching fish. The flash, on the other hand, was well stocked. It had much more to offer and I had ignored the canal.

Now at last I had to fish the canal. But Wilf Dyson, the truest of friends, told me he wasn't fishing himself and that he was lending me all his tackle—some of the best in the district. Wilf also had the full range of baits and groundbait. Even though this was thirty years ago local anglers had been breeding gozzers—those extra-special hook maggots—for years. They weren't called gozzers, we called them dumpies, but these clever Leigh anglers were a long way ahead of the field in knowledge.

So I went to this match fully equipped. I was the equal of every other angler in quality of bait and tackle. There were over 200 men fishing and I drew peg number nine. My swim was three pegs away from a wide basin and one or two men advised me how to fish it.

They suggested I should lay the bait a yard on to the bottom but after an hour—of this two-hour match—I was fishless. And there had been very few fish caught anywhere. I heard the chatter of the anglers along the line and it seemed as though weights were going to be very low.

I decided to change to the style I had always used on the flash. Instead of leaving the bait down on the bottom I brought it up so that is was just off the bottom. I put some very fine groundbait and a few squatts in on the little and often principle.

After feeding and fishing in this way for five minutes I caught my first fish—a 5 oz. roach. For the remaining period of the match I caught a further eight roach and took the top weight. I weighed in 1 lb. 14 oz. and the next weight, for the man who came second, was 14 oz. Considering I had wasted half the time fishing a style I had been told was the right one and had then changed over to what was then my natural method, I felt very happy. I knew that if I had fished my own style the whole time I would have topped the 3 lb. mark.

The only sad note about this match was that I missed the bookie! I had been on the small match pools but I hadn't realised what the bookie had meant when he asked me if I was having a go. So I missed my first opportunity to win some money. But I must give the bookie his due. He treated me well afterwards, as well he might— for I had spared him having to pay the winner!

This was the real beginning of my match fishing, but that afternoon there was a further match on another section of the canal. I went to that and won again. I again used my flash style and caught a lot of little rudd which totalled close to 2 lb. I won easily.

This was in October and the main club contests locally had already been fished that year. The colder weather soon puts canal fish off the feed and, traditionally, fixtures were concluded before the bad weather came.

But during the winter months I fished the canal at every chance I had. There was a warm water outfall from Plank Lane Colliery which ran into the Leigh Canal and I fished close to that warm patch all through the winter. My two wins had made me so keen that I was determined to practise all I could and to be ready for the next season.

At that time few anglers fished in the winter. I used to creep quietly to the water for I didn't want other people to see me. They would have thought that I must have been stupid to fish at that time of the year. But I steadily accumulated knowledge that was to stand me in good stead the following summer.

That summer came and I won all eight of the Fir Tree club

matches and I also won the club's big match of the year on the Fir Tree flash. In addition I also took first place in a number of the club's sweepstake matches.

That year the diehard members of the club continued fishing through the winter for the first time, fishing the warm water section of the canal. And that was really how winter fishing began in this section of Lancashire.

Having done very well with the Fir Tree club I then realised that I had to look further afield for stronger opposition. I decided to join the Leigh Angling Society. It was a smaller club than the Fir Tree but the standard of skill among its members was even higher than in the Fir Tree.

The very first time I fished with the Leigh Society I won. In fact I won all four club contests and the annual big match as well. During this time I had begun to breed my own specials for hookbait in the summer months. I reared my own feeder maggots too. And Wilf Dyson had given me his rod, the one I used to win that very first canal match. In return I told Wilf when he gave me the rod that I would give him the very first gold medal I ever won in a fishing match—if I ever won one.

Success followed success in local fishing and as time passed I moved further afield for my matches. Instead of restricting myself to local canals I fished flowing rivers like the Weaver. I even travelled to the Severn on a number of occasions and, at times, got into the prize list.

But the war intervened. This didn't stop fishing altogether but, with the coming of rationing, groundbaiting was out. What could previously be used for feeding fish was now more important for feeding cattle and even the human population.

I still carried on fishing as and when I could, but although I was a coal miner and in a reserved occupation many of the local matchmen were drawn into the three services. Competition continued but at a much reduced level.

To supplement the few scraps of bread I could obtain for fishing, I turned to using what is now known as black magic. This fine leaf mould, riddled very fine and laced with squatts, proved as successful as groundbait at attracting fish.

There were still big matches fished at local level. The National Championship was cancelled for the duration of the war but at that time I was still only on the fringes of big national competition. The temporary abandonment of the National didn't seem of any importance.

During the war I won some matches but there were limited

opportunities for match fishing. Transport was the difficulty. There was no petrol for pleasure.

Even so I found my way to the Ribble, the Lune, the Weaver and the Wyre; all North-west waters, where I steadily built up my knowledge of how to fish. Practice is the most important aspect of match fishing and even though I wasn't making a name for myself I was at least improving and making ready for the time when large-scale nation-wide competitions resumed.

Tackle was difficult to obtain and this was to prove a great advantage in some respects. I had to make my own rods and also reached the stage when I had to tie my own hooks. I was then able to fully realise the value of making specialist tackle for specific purposes.

Even after the war groundbaiting restrictions remained in force for some time. But in 1946, immediately after the end of the war, I qualified to fish my first National Championship. This was on the River Trent and I fished for the Freshwater Fish Preservation League. At that time I had never seen the Trent, much less fished it.

I went to this National with the finest possible bait and rods but with wartime shortages plaguing the fishing tackle trade—and nylon line still not with us—I had to use an inferior line. This was to prove costly. My line let me down and in addition I didn't have the right hooks for the water. The latter was hardly surprising, never having seen the Trent before, but I had the good fortune to draw a top class peg.

I fished well out into the stream with a fourteen foot rod at the time when the Trent tactics by local anglers were to use a nine foot rod and to fish close to the near bank. I used my own style of long casting to keep my tackle well away from other anglers since this had always stood me in good stead on canals and on the Fir Tree flash.

My peg was below Newark in a section where there were lots of chub. I didn't land one of them but I was broken up by big fish on six occasions. Each time they took away my terminal tackle and I weighed in just over 10 lb. of small fish—dace and roach. The match was won with 16 lb. and the second man had 12 lb. I finished in around seventh position but had I landed those chub I would have doubled my weight—and won easily.

This was experience the hard way. It taught me the value of having the right tackle for the job. If I had been using a top quality line I would have landed those chub. Thus my first chance of success in really big-time match fishing was lost.

I missed the boat that day. I have fished every National Championship bar two since that Trent match but I have never had the same chance again. I missed one match as the result of injuries sustained in a car crash and was unable to fish the Witham in 1951, the year Sam Buxton won it. But I have never drawn another peg which gave me as good a chance of winning. That remains my unfulfilled ambition. There is no higher honour than winning the National Championship and, so far at least, this has eluded me.

No-one can ever hope to win the National Championship without a degree of luck. Matches can be won at average pegs but in a contest where 1,200 and more anglers are competing the winner has to have a good peg. There is, of course, more than one potentially winning peg in every National. There are men who have had chances to win and have never known it—even to this day. They hadn't tackled up right, they had fed wrong, their bait hadn't been right.

For any one of these reasons, or for many others, they failed. Match fishing is now of a much higher standard than it has ever been before but the first essential piece of good fortune must be in getting a favourable peg. With the exception of that Trent match I have never been in with a chance of winning a National Championship.

In the main my local fishing had always been roach fishing. The local water gave me no opportunity to fish for bream. It wasn't until as late as 1960 that I first began to take an active interest in bream fishing and in the big open contests that are fished each year on such popular match rivers as the Welland and the Witham.

But I had theories of my own. On Fir Tree flash I had practised fishing at long range. There, and on reservoirs at Chorley, I practised fishing with a sliding float and also legered under all conditions. I practised the bream fishing techniques even though I could only catch roach. Thus I was at least partially equipped for the time when I fished a big match in a bream river. If I was drawn into a swim that held bream I would be able to catch them.

I have now spent thousands of hours fishing the Witham—the river I believe the best bream river of them all. I have had some wonderful catches of fish, having taken 40 lb. catches. Technically I am well equipped to fish the river but I haven't had the best of luck at the draw. It is one of those odd quirks of fate that although I have often finished well up in the prize lists I have never had a win there.

My main success has come when fishing for roach. I have done well in the Trent, the Weaver, and in Welbeck Lakes. My biggest win so far was when I won the Northern Anglers Championship with 1,300 anglers fishing in 1948. That was on the Lancaster Canal at Garstang. I had 3 lb. 14 oz. of small roach—119 fish.

I have not fished Welbeck Lakes very often but these waters hold an abundance of good-class roach. Up to the time of writing I have won seven of the nineteen matches I have fished there. I hold the record for weight of fish in a three-hour match, taking 17 lb. of roach from the small lake in 1962. That was in a contest fished by 500 anglers. In addition I have had three seconds and have never yet been lower than tenth.

My main satisfaction has been that I have won with big weights. I had 20 lb. in one five-hour contest and have mostly topped the 10 lb. mark. In 1967 I was second in the match that was the first one to be fished there after disease had led to the lakes being closed to fishing for a time. I drew a good peg in the middle lake. But the near edge was fringed with thick weed for eighteen feet. Each time I hooked a big roach I was in trouble. I couldn't lift it up and slide it over the weeds to the landing net. There was no problem with the smaller ones, but I must have lost a dozen roach of 1 lb. or better. I weighed in 13 lb. 7 oz. and the winner just topped the 14 lb. mark!

The Trent has been another of my happy hunting grounds. It is a great river but a long way from my home and I don't get there as often as I would like to do. In addition there are not a great number of open matches that I, and others like me, can fish.

I was second in the Club and Institute National there in 1961 with 19 lb. 11 oz. and won the Nottingham versus Manchester (fifty a side) event in 1961 with 17 lb. 8 oz., winning by a very wide margin.

I can claim responsibility for introducing caster fishing to the Trent and other rivers. Lots of anglers have misunderstood this caster fishing, saying they have fished with chrysalids for years. They claimed that caster fishing was nothing new. What was new about caster fishing was that the maggot chrysalids were conditioned so that they would sink. Most chrysalids used as hook maggots were previously 'floaters'. Thus, under the new technique, casters could be used as sinking feed and this proved extremely successful on many other rivers as well as on the Trent.

The stick float was another of my inventions. I brought it out for use in canals when catching fish 'on the drop'—when fishing near the far bank and when the fish were taking a falling bait. The tip of the float is of balsa and the stem is made of the heavy Tonkin cane. Its essential properties are that it sets very quickly in the water and registers bites that can come almost as soon as the float hits the water after the cast has been made.

In the course of thirty years of match fishing I have won a huge number of contests. They vary between small sweepstakes and giant open events and I have never kept an accurate account of their numbers. In Lancashire alone I estimate I have won eighty open matches and the full total for all events must run to 300.

B

My biggest cash win was the £110 I collected in the Norther
Anglers Championship on the Lancaster Canal. I haven't kept a
accurate account of the prize moneys won from all matches but th
figure must run to several thousands of pounds—and much of thi
total was made when cash prizes were very much smaller than the
are now. But at first sight this may be considered a large sum c
money and there are people who would accuse me of being nothin
more nor less than a professional angler.

But the money received in prizes is only one side of the story. I
costs a lot of money to fish all over the country these days. Takin
travelling, bait, pools, tackle and other expenditure into account
costs about three pounds to fish the average match. In some instance:
involving big pools and greater distance, the cost could be as hig
as eight pounds. National Championships involve an even highe
outlay and, with everything included, can run to as much as fiftee
pounds.

From this it can be seen that the profit margin is quite slim an
indeed the average angler is hard put to it to continue fishing matche
week after week unless he has the occasional win.

From these facts it must be crystal clear that the match angler—
while keen to win what cash he can—fishes for much more than th
material benefits. Match angling is a test of skill and whether yo
play golf, darts, football or whatever it is, every man wants to be
winner in his chosen pastime. This gives him great personal satis
faction and a sense of achievement—which is what my success ha
given me.

Match fishing is also a social thing. If only before and after th
events anglers enjoy each other's company. It is not all cut and thrus
and highly-serious competition. There is a section of the greate
angling community which maintains that match fishing is wrong an
should be banned. They maintain that their own approach to th
sport—probably fishing for big fish all the time—is the right one.

But it isn't as simple as that. If every man wanted to fish for bi
fish all the time half the rivers in this country would never be fishe
at all, for they do not hold any number of top-quality fish. Thu
match anglers can make use of relatively poor waters for competitio
fishing, ensuring that the greatest possible recreation is obtaine
from all the waters in this country.

It has sometimes been said that match anglers are basically tiddle
snatchers. That they are not interested in catching big fish. Eve
that they would cut their lines if they hooked something big that too
a lot of time to land. This is complete nonsense!

Every match angler fishes with the intention of getting the greates possible weight of fish from the swim in front of him. If there are big fish there he must try for them—if they are likely to feed. There are many occasions when matchmen have no alternative but to go for little fish simply because the bigger fish are either not there at all or are not feeding. But in all circumstances matchmen go for the bigger fish when there is a reasonable chance of getting them. How else can they hope to get the best weight of the day?

I shall be a match angler for as long as I am physically capable of continuing. There are a number of ambitions still to be fulfilled and the main one is, of course, to win the National Championship. I may never win it but failure will not be for want of effort.

2. Making a Match Angler

THERE IS NO SUCH THING as a born angler. Every man is as good a fisherman as he makes himself. True some men seem to have an ability to absorb and acquire knowledge much quicker than others, but everyone has to start at the bottom. There was a time when many successful men used to keep all their knowledge as secret as possible but I have always enjoyed helping and advising beginners to improve their skill. I was helped and now I must do what I can to help others.

There is no short cut to ability. Fishing has to begin with the basics and is then improved and practised through the years. Many budding match anglers become discouraged too quickly, simply because they expect too much of themselves. I have based all my own contest fishing on years of practice and one is no use without the other.

Take the National Championship for example. Each year the contest is fished on a different river. The men who fish this match are the best from their respective angling associations. But in many many cases they have no experience either of the venue itself or of another river like it. Thus, although they may be quite skilled at fishing techniques and application in their local rivers, they are at a grave disadvantage when fishing elsewhere. They go off to the National full of high hopes and great expectations only to find they have no chance of catching enough fish to put them anywhere near the top.

These anglers have put the cart before the horse. They should have obtained pre-match information about the venue and have fished it themselves a number of times. I know this isn't always possible but if the actual river cannot be fished in advance then the angler must find as near a carbon-copy of it as exists. Thus he will be aware of the problems he will have to face on match day and have the knowledge to enable him to put up a good performance.

The Fir Tree flash has been my Witham and my Welland, my Welbeck and my Weaver. It isn't an exact replica of those four rivers of course it's not, but I have been able to practise the techniques that have to be used on all four of those rivers. The flash is deep in parts shallow in others. Each section of bank represents problems and

have never gone to it simply to sit down and try to catch 40 lb. of fish.

I have fished every swim in that water, which has the capacity for about 150 pegs. It varies in depth from five to sixteen feet. And I have fished each of those pegs under every possible set of circumstances. I have deliberately sat down to face a strong wind, knowing this would reduce my catch on the day but knowing too that by mastering it I would increase my knowledge of how to catch fish under difficult conditions.

I have legered and I have float-fished. I have float-legered and gone through all the permutations of fishing theory. I have tried each and every sensible bait, colour of bait and various types of groundbait and methods of groundbaiting. I have experimented with lines and hooks and even now am attempting to find a new method of legering which will allow anglers to take roach from streamy water when the water temperature is low. At such times, the fish want a bait presented still on the bottom. They will not chase and take a bait moving with the flow.

This was clearly demonstrated on the Trent in the 1966/67 winter but the popular methods of legering widely used today are not good enough. Too many bites are missed and I am searching for a method which will give me a fish from every bite.

Early indications are encouraging and I may have the answer. I don't know yet but I shall continue to experiment on this and many other aspects of fishing. For a match angler must have an enquiring mind. He must be able to see the problem and then work out a solution. Whether the problems are worked at by individuals or by groups of anglers is immaterial, but it is only by studying the present day problems that we can find the answers.

And, of course, it is the man or men who find the answers first who win the matches. True they don't keep their secrets for long but at least they do well for a time until others copy them. Then they have to keep one jump ahead by turning to something else that will give them the advantage over their opponents.

The angler's object must be to hook a fish every time he gets a bite and that means getting a fish every time his bait is mouthed. When an angler retrieves his tackle to find a sucked maggot on the hook he is fishing badly. He had a chance to hook a fish and missed it.

Therefore each man must analyse his day's fishing and look for the errors in it. Missed bites stem from many many reasons—as does the failure to get bites at all. No single aspect of match fishing is too small to demand intense analysis and a determination to find a better and quicker way of hooking fish.

I have always been very thorough in this way and strongly advise everyone else to be the same. I have won 300 matches but so can you—if you go about it in the right way.

Single-mindedness is essential. Every second of each contest demands that the angler be keyed up to catching fish and not slumped in resignation waiting for the whistle to end what has been a bad day. We all get shocking pegs. Pegs where we know we haven't the slightest chance of winning. But if those pegs pose problems they can at least help us to exercise our minds and find the answers. We won't always be successful but at least we shall have tried—and we may learn something which will be of use in a better swim another time.

To be a top-class match angler demands physical fitness. Maybe this doesn't seem so important to an angler as to an athlete but a full box of tackle is heavy and often has to be carried long distances. Therefore the man who gets to his peg in good condition is much better equipped to start fishing than someone who sits puffing and blowing for the first ten minutes. That time could be better employed in assessing the swim and preparing for the match itself.

Staying power is also important. Just because a man has a long walk to his peg doesn't mean that he can jettison half his groundbait to make the walk easier. Anglers must be prepared to carry everything they are likely to need.

I well remember walking almost two miles to a peg on the Calder in 1964. The ground was hard and it was a difficult walk. I had to prepare the spot from which I was to fish so that I could have all my tackle close to hand. I then had to sit down and fish for six hours. I caught 40 lb. 5 oz. of fish that day. It was a match of heavy weights and I couldn't afford to relax and say I had caught enough. Therefore concentration and staying power are essential factors in match-fishing success.

Poor eyesight can be a great disadvantage and it is one disability that cannot be overcome. But even anglers with really fine eyesight can improve their chances by minimising the strain they will be called upon to face in a long match. Sunglasses and eye-shades cut the glare out of the sun and reduce the problem of spotting the tip of a float on a choppy surface. Excessive eyestrain leads to headaches, physical discomfort and fewer fish.

Nothing is too small to be given consideration, for the accumulative effect of a number of small disadvantages and inconveniences can easily lead to lost opportunity.

Confidence is all-important. One of the values of practice fishing is that if an angler catches a big weight of fish on a particular method he goes to a match knowing that what he has done once he can do again. So, practice can build confidence as well as technical ability.

Without confidence there is little point in fishing any match. Confidence is bred of knowledge of one's own ability. A lot of young match anglers start fishing the really big open events too soon. It costs them a lot of money which would be better spent on longer periods of practice fishing. By beginning before they are really completely ready, they wreck their own confidence and have difficulty in getting it back. My advice is to never fish any match you do not honestly feel you have some chance of winning.

This psychological attitude is invaluable. But it is born of the ability to handle tackle properly and of having the right bait—and enough of it—for the job in hand.

But confidence has to be based on knowledge and an individual would probably have difficulty making himself a top-class matchman solely by his own efforts. There is a shortcut by watching anglers who often do well. There are many points that can be picked up in this way. Watching is not the complete answer, obviously it cannot be. But having watched what a crack angler does to overcome a certain problem it is a simple matter to return to your own fishing and apply the lessons learned.

It's a hard road and it's a long one but there are very few keen novices who couldn't become top-class matchmen if they made the effort.

3. Rods, Reels, Lines and Hooks

Rods

THERE CAN BE no economy with tackle for match anglers who want
to do well, but at the same time the most expensive items in the various
ranges are not necessarily the best. They may, in fact, be the best for
one man and not for another. Each man has to find out for himself
what tackle he can handle best. A man of six feet three inches may,
for example, find he can handle a fifteen foot rod with ease, but the
short chap should never imagine that just because this big fellow
does well with a long rod that he can do the same.

Hollow fibre-glass rods have made a huge impact on match
angling. They have superseded the brittle Spanish reel rods used ten
years ago. Glass, a man-made substance, does not lose its strength,
is much more reliable and can be produced in any size or taper to
give the angler the qualities he expects from his rod.

As I see it, glass has everything in its favour. In its earlier days it
was prone to sloppiness, affecting casting and striking, but as a
greater variety of tapers have become available to the fishing tackle
trade so these difficulties have largely been overcome.

Each angler finds out the length of the rod that suits him best.
have a great preference for a rod of twelve feet six inches. I never find
I need a longer one simply because I never find it necessary to cast a
fixed float in very deep water. I would always use a sliding float in
situations like this. The anglers who prefer to cast a fixed float at
depths of twelve feet and over must, of course, use longer rods, but
have grave doubts as to whether this is as efficient as using a sliding
float and shorter rod.

My ideal rod is a three-piece. I need a rod with an all-through
action. This is important today, now that many anglers are turning
over to fishing at long range. The old Spanish reed rods were stiff
through the butt and middle joints, having action, casting power if
you like, in the tip. Those rods would not be so efficient for long
casting as modern glass rods.

I think three joints are enough. Four-joint rods mean an extra
ferrule, and even with the lightweight ferrules in use these days, the

adds some weight and stiffens the middle of the rod, taking away some of the casting power.

Anglers can buy their own blanks and make up spare butts for existing rods, thus being able to reduce them in length. It is vital to have a spare rod but, as I see it, both rods can be identical. A short butt can be made up and used for leger fishing. When using a butt-bite indicator I find eight feet is the best length, but a swingtip rod is a specialist tool.

I do not care for the swingtips which can be screwed into a threaded end ring on the rod tip. These tend to unscrew in use. Swingtip rods —with the tip permanently attached—are quite cheap and good ones can be bought for as little as £4 10s. A big ring on the butt is a useful aid to casting.

One useful innovation available today is the fined-down tip used for direct legering from the rod top. This is extremely useful in the faster-flowing and deep rivers, where the sheer strength of the flow makes either a swingtip or a butt-bite indicator useless. The tip sets to the pull of the stream but still retains enough sensitivity to give adequate bite indications. These tips may have to be fitted by the angler himself to some rods but the great standardisation apparent in rod design means that tips can be bought 'off the shelf' for most rods.

It is rather silly to economise when buying a rod. But while the very cheap rods should be ignored, there is good value for money in rods selling at anything between £8 to £10. But the more expensive rods usually incorporate better-quality rings, higher-grade cork on the handles and even higher-quality glass itself. Thus there is much less likelihood of these letting you down at a vital stage in a contest.

There are many suitable match rods available and these are perfectly satisfactory. But the rod is not the most important piece of equipment. Whether or not the angler is successful depends on other items of tackle and in the way these are used, rather than in the perfect rod.

Reels

This is the age of the fixed-spool reel—and with good reason. Anything that the centre-pin reel can do the fixed spool can be made to do equally well—with practice. And in most points the fixed spool has everything in its favour.

Some anglers hold that the traditional use of a centre-pin reel for long trotting close to the near bank cannot be rivalled. I disagree with this, finding the fixed spool its equal. Indeed young anglers taking up fishing for the first time need never bother with a centre-pin at all. The reel was a good one for some purposes but is now obsolete.

The fixed spool allows distance casting with great accuracy and very little weight. The centre-pin has to be worked with the fingers and is seriously handicapped by windy conditions. The latest retrieve rate of the newer fixed-spool reels is such that the one feature centre-pin anglers might have claimed as a point in their favour has been swept aside.

The French reel, which has dominated the British market since the war, continues to be the best available. The manufacturers appear to have studied the market very closely and have taken care to introduce the necessary refinements seen to be needed for match fishing.

Too many reels are complicated in that their spools cannot be removed quickly. The press stud type of release gives a terrific advantage in time saved when an angler has the misfortune to get the line behind the spool.

One critical point I would make—and this applies to every reel on the market today—is that manufacturers still insist on giving us spools with too much depth. Some require a ridiculous amount of line to fill them.

Strictly, no match angler needs more than 100 yards of line on a spool, and it will be a most progressive step when we can buy spools needing no more line than that to fill them. To get over this problem I always build up my spools with sheet cork, leaving sufficient space for 100 yards of line. See Fig. 1. Care must be taken not to build

FIG. 1

The spool of a fixed-spool reel built up with three layers of $\frac{1}{16}$ in. sheet cork. A hundred yards of line then completely fills the spool and there is a reduced amount of friction on the spool lip, ensuring good casting. The amount of cork used depends on the thickness of the line

the spools up too high or the line will come off in loops during casting. A full spool is a great aid to casting since this reduces the friction of the line rubbing on the rim of the spool.

Another important point is the weight of the reel. I prefer a light one. Remember the reel is not placed at the end of the butt where its weight will be partially offset by the leverage and weight of the rod. The reel is seated under the hand and the angler has to hold the weight of the reel all the while he is fishing.

Reels should always be adequately greased and lubricated so that they function properly. And the line spool must receive constant attention. In particular the top edge of the spool should be cleaned regularly. A speck of mud or groundbait can harden to the rim of the spool and then badly upset casting. I keep the casting rim of my spools highly polished to minimise friction during casting.

Lines

I carry three reel spools in my fishing basket. They hold lines of 1½ lb. breaking strain, 2.6 lb. breaking strain and 3 lb. breaking strain respectively. I never use a heavier line than 3 lb., for I am sure this will deal with any fish I am likely to catch in a match. After all, I don't expect to run into big carp and rarely fish rivers containing barbel.

And although I have the 3 lb. line I very rarely use it. Even when legering I find the 2.6 lb. better. It is finer and the bites register better with that than with heavier line.

The 1½ lb. line is used in canals, where fine lines are essential. There are also many occasions when I find that breaking strain quite adequate for the Trent. It is particularly useful on windless days, but even when good roach are feeding fast I have never known the line to break either on the strike or when playing a fish. It has snapped when snagged on the bottom, but that can happen to any line.

The 2.6 line is used on the Severn when I am never quite sure how big the next fish may be. It could be a 5 lb. chub and I want to be able to deal with it. This is also the reel line I use when fishing a sliding float on the wide bream rivers of Fenland.

My 3 lb. line is the reserve for use at times when the bank and bottom are bad. Using this I can apply maximum pressure and there is a good chance of pulling free without breaking. I find it best to fish with as fine a line as possible on all occasions. The smaller diameter means longer, easier and more accurate casting. There is less effort and the result is better fishing.

There are scores of different brands of line on the market today. I have my favourite and no doubt you have yours. I am perfectly satisfied with the brand of monofilament nylon I use and would not change it for any other. Yet there are anglers who would disagree with my choice and tell me they have never had any trouble with such and such a brand. I suppose the main thing is to be confident that whatever line you use is capable of dealing with the situation in which you are using it. Some anglers have unfairly criticised a line when they have been fishing too fine and have been clearly asking for trouble.

My requirement of a line is firstly that it should be of the strength credited to it. Most are. But I also want a line which can be made to sink easily. Few lines will do that, so I never wind a new line straight off the spool and on to the reel. I first soak it overnight in hot soapy water, weighting the spool down into the water so that it is totally submerged.

This makes the line more supple and a further advantage is that a proportion of the water is absorbed into the line. This makes it easier to sink. There is nothing worse than using a line that will not sink when cast across the width of a wide river on a windy day. The line must be sunk at once or the float will be dragged out of position. I sink the top of the rod under the surface and then complete two quick turns on the reel handle to retrieve line. This, and the action of whipping the rod top sideways to surface level, should be sufficient to sink the full length of the line.

A sunken line is, of course, essential when fishing with a float which is fastened to the line by the base ring only. Another useful remedy for a floating line is to wind it in along the striking edge of a safety-match box. I must emphasise that this must be done with great care or the line will be damaged. But, by winding the line in along the striking edge, the shiny surface of the line is rubbed off and is then able to absorb water more quickly—and will soon sink.

As I mentioned when talking about reels, I like to have no more than 100 yards of line on a spool. But care has to be taken to see that there is always enough line on the spool before starting to fish. A couple of breaks when fishing at long range and there isn't much line left. It pays to check that there is at least fifty yards remaining on the spool. If there is less, then a further break will mean there is not enough line left to be able to carry on fishing—with that particular spool anyway.

It is said that some nylon lines deteriorate when kept on a reel spool. They may, I don't know, for I never use any line long enough to find this out. There are very few days of the season when I do not go fishing and the average line lasts me no more than six weeks.

Hooks

Ever since I first started fishing I have tied my own hooks. In the early days I used to use fine strands of silk for the whippings, completing the operation with glue. I was taught to do this by the top-ranking anglers of the North West and always considered that I could tie better than I could buy.

After the war however the spade-end hook was imported into this country in huge numbers. The spade was always much too large for my taste and even today I cut most of this off with a pair of fine pliers. I leave only a tiny flange of pressed wire to prevent the knot from slipping off the shank.

Many men are perfectly happy with the simple spade-end knot but I am more exacting. I still prefer the traditional method of hook tying. I whip each hook with twelve turns of silk and give the whipping a single coat of glue afterwards. But I take one important precaution so that the nylon does not pull through my whipping. I tie a single knot in that part of the hook length which is to be whipped on

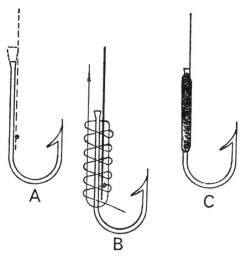

FIG. 2

Benny Ashurst's method of whipping a spade-end hook. Drawing (A) shows the amount of spade-end cut off with pliers and the hook bottom in position for whipping. (B) shows the whipping Benny uses and (C) the finished article after the whipping has been coated with glue

to the hook shank. Thus if the hook length is to be pulled away from the hook the whole of the whipping has also to be pulled free—and this is extremely unlikely. See Fig. 2.

Proprietry brands of glue can be bought in tubes to dress the hook whippings but I think these adhesives are too thick and are best thinned down with amyl acetate, which can be bought at any chemist's. When thinned down the glue spreads evenly along the whipping, glazing it evenly. I apply the glue with a pointed matchstick. I have never known hooks tied in this way to pull off the shank and can use them with the utmost confidence.

One disadvantage of those large spades is that when retrieving at speed the resistance of the water on the spade starts the bait revolving. This causes twisting of the hook length and also puts turns into the line itself and is the reason why I clip my spades.

By general standards I suppose the hooks I use are very small. But I have no fixed ideas and will always vary the size of the hook in accordance with the bait being used. If, for instance, I were fishing for bream in Ireland with lobworms I would have no hesitation about using a size 6 hook. But most of my fishing is maggot and caster fishing, often on waters where the fish are heavily fished-for and shy. Therefore I find the smaller range of hooks is vital.

I never use a gilt hook. To my mind these show up too clearly in the water and I cannot forget the words of an old hook-maker who once told me that not only were gilts thicker in the shank but also that they were an inferior hook. I have always preferred the bronze and blued hooks. When hooks were difficult to obtain during the war, the old hook-maker I have just mentioned used to send me some he made himself. These were patterned on what was once known as the Wigan bloodworm round bend. This really was a top-class product and was widely used in Lancashire.

It is easy to become confused by the variety of hook shapes available today but my choice is very simple. I stick to the round bend varieties—whether I fish with maggots, caster, bread or worm.

I see no advantage in having a variety of the different shapes of hook. To stick rigidly to one particular pattern makes it a simple matter to stock my basket and I do not suffer from confusion of choice.

I never use a hook smaller than a size 20. When I am baiting with a single pinkie or even a single squatt I find the 20 plenty small enough. I tie this size hook to an eighteen inch length of 1 lb. breaking strain nylon.

As far as I am concerned the 18 is the most popular hook. I tie it to 1 lb. breaking strain for canal fishing and to 1½ lb. for river fishing for bream and roach. As my hook sizes increase so I progressively use stronger line on which to tie them. For the size 16 I use 2 lb. line and only occasionally 1½ lb. The size 14 is tied to 2 lb. and 2½ lb. The 12 is tied to 3 lb. and even bigger hooks than this can be safely tied on 3 lb. line.

For maggot fishing I prefer the size range from 20 to size 12, for bread fishing from 14 to 12 and for worms from 14 up to size 6—depending on the size of the worm. The only time I use a really big hook is when bream fishing in Ireland.

I tie all my hooks to eighteen inch hook lengths. I dislike both

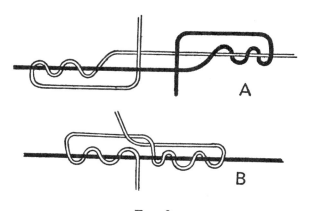

FIG. 3
The bloodknot used for attaching (A) hook lengths and
(B) leger links to the reel line

yard bottoms and the shorter twelve inch lengths to which so many hooks are tied. My objection to the yard is that if the tackle fouls bottom and breaks off, some of the shot are lost and have to be replaced. It is much quicker to merely have to replace the hook and to have the shot intact each time. The twelve inch bottoms are too short, for they reduce the natural suppleness of the line at the crucial point where the bait is presented to the fish. They can make a bait look unnatural to a fish.

I prefer to knot my hook lengths to the reel line rather than use the popular double loop method. Those double loops pick up too much rubbish to my way of thinking and, of course, there are two knots instead of just the one. I use the bloodknot shown in Fig. 3A to join the hook length to the reel line.

I never save the hook after the end of one day's fishing even though it may be in good condition. I like to be very fussy about the quality of each hook I use and even before tying I examine them with a magnifying glass to pick out any that may be below standard. I reject any with inferior barbs and points.

4. Floats

THERE IS A CONFUSION of choice of floats on the market. Many anglers are tempted into buying one or two whenever they go into a tackle shop, thus increasing the numbers they have and will probably never use.

Each float I have in my tackle box is a specialist float made for a certain function. I know exactly what to expect of it, how it will behave due to the properties of the material from which it is made, its casting power, how it holds up and its exact shot-carrying capacity.

I don't have a single float in my box that I have bought from a tackle shop. I am certain that I can make much better floats than I can buy. And part of the pleasure in fishing, for me at least, is to consider the problems posed by a certain river and then to design floats capable of combating the problems of that river.

Most of my success in canal fishing has come by casting to and fishing near the far bank. And the bites have come while the bait is

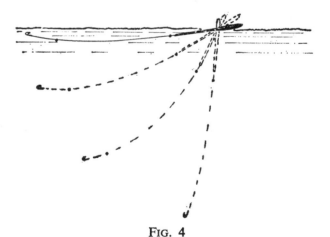

FIG. 4

The stick float cocking after being cast. Note that whenever a fish takes the bait this must register on the float, giving the angler a perfect indication of the bite

still falling through the water immediately after the cast. Thus I wa
a float that will gradually tilt and settle to the pull of the shot on th
line. It must be in register with the shot and tell me when a fish
taking. See Fig. 4.

I found the answer to be the stick float, which has proved s
popular all over the country. I designed this float some twelve yea
ago, when I hit on the idea that a buoyant top and a heavy ba
incorporated into a float would provide this pendulum action. Th
buoyancy of the balsa in the tip holds it up to the surface while th
heavy cane sinks through the water in an arc. I found that hig
density Tonkin cane was the best material for the base.

By varying the length and diameter of the balsa in the tip in relatic
to the cane I was able to make a number of floats with a variety
shot-carrying capacities. This range extends from a minimum of

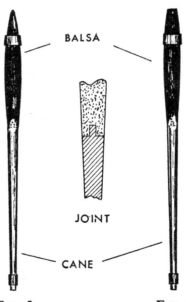

FIG. 5   FIG. 6

The stick float used for still or slow-moving water.
This is shotted so that the tip merely peeps above the
surface (*Fig. 5*). The stick float for faster water. The
blunt tip allows the float to combat turbulence and flow
without being pulled under the surface (*Fig. 6*). Both
floats are fastened to the line by two pieces of valve
rubber.

ingle BB and one dust shot up to one AAA and a dust shot. See Fig. 5.

When shotting for canal fishing I place the BB tight up under the loat and the single dust shot is placed on to the line a foot from the hook. The BB shot is up near the float simply to add to the weight and to increase casting power. The same float could also be used on a flowing river like the Trent, but in that case the shotting would be different. Instead of placing the BB under the float I split that weight into either three No. 6 or two No. 4 shot and space these equidistant along the length of line below the float.

Trent fishing doesn't usually entail casting more than three rod lengths out and therefore there is no need for that extra shot near the float. Instead, the weight is placed further down below the float to allow the bait to be presented in a natural fall, thus offsetting the effect of the speed of the flow of the river on the bait. See Fig. 7.

It is a simple matter to learn the behaviour pattern of this float after it has been cast. It is possible to time the float's movements as it cocks and any variation from the usual must bring a prompt response. Whenever the float either dips sharply or fails to settle in the normal way a fish is usually responsible. The strike is made at once and a fish is hooked.

I shape these stick floats so that the balsa tip which protrudes above the surface has been sharpened down almost as fine as a pencil point. Thus the amount of float above the surface is very small indeed and bites register instantly.

The length of these floats varies between six and nine inches, the depth of the water being the factor dictating the final choice. If the canal is a mere eighteen inches deep then I use the shorter float, whereas I use the longer one on the Trent where the depth is greater. The thickness of the floats can be varied so that both the long and short floats have the same shot-carrying capacity.

These stick floats must be fished what I call 'double rubbered'. That means being fastened to the line both at the top and bottom. When bites are being registered 'on the drop', to fasten at the base only upsets the pendulum action of the float and its advantages are lost. And, of course, there is a further advantage in this double rubber fishing for it means the float can be changed at will, either for a different size or for one with a different coloured tip if the light should have changed.

If I am fishing with a shot tripping the bottom of the river I prefer to use a stick float with a blunt tip. This shape of float has greater buoyancy in the tip and this helps it to hold up to the surface instead of dragging under with the flow. See Fig. 6.

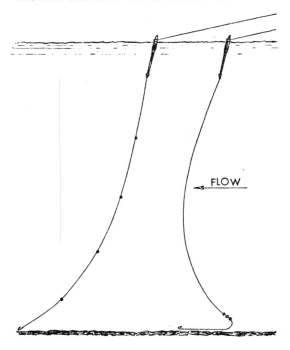

FLOW

FIG. 7

The right and wrong ways to shot a stick float when fishing the River Trent. When the shot are spaced out evenly between the float and the hook, bites register very much better than when the shot are bunched. There is less slack line and the hook is in direct register with the float

In recent years on the drop fishing hasn't proved quite so succe ful. The roach have gone off the feed for long periods and a falli bait hasn't produced so many bites. Sometimes the bait has had be fished on the bottom and this requires a very different float to stick float. The stick is a good float for a falling bait but it nothing to counteract the surface drift often evident on canals.

The float I have brought out for this purpose is made from peacc quill. It is in two parts, with a thin inset into the top of the lov half. The float measures between four and five inches overall—w the varied lengths allowing for different shot-carrying capaciti The peacock inset extends to an inch and a half. The advantage this fine tip is that it enables better casting than would a single length of quill. I aim for a shot-load of three BB and one No. 4. The float is fastened to the line by running the line through the small base ring. One BB shot is nipped on the line above the float and the remaining two just below it, trapping the float in position. The No. 4 is positioned a foot from the hook. See Fig. 8.

The fact that this float takes more shot than the stick float and that it is fastened at one end only, instead of top and bottom, helps it to overcome the surface drift problem. The object must be to sink the line quickly, for otherwise the float will still be carried away with the drift. Once the line is sunk the float remains stationary.

One very important point: once the BB shot have been nipped on

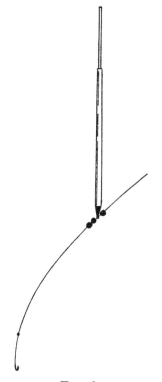

FIG. 8

The two-piece peacock-quill float used for fishing a bait on the bottom of canals. The float is locked in position by the shot (as shown)

to the line they hold the float in position. But if the depth has to be altered the shot have to be moved. Therefore I have to use the softest shot I can get so that it opens easily. To facilitate this change of depth with the minimum waste of time I nick a vee into each shot at the split with a razor blade. I can then press my thumb-nail into the vee and the shot opens at once. This wouldn't be possible either without the vee or with hard shot. See Fig. 9.

One of the latest floats to prove popular in the North West is made

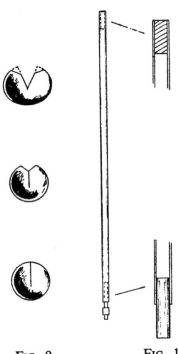

Fig. 9   Fig. 10

The advantages of nicking an additional vee into split shot with a razor blade. When this has been done shot nipped on to the line is easily opened with the thumb-nail. If the shot is used without this extra vee it takes much more time to open and remove (*Fig. 9*). A float made from a plastic drinking straw. The tip is plugged with peacock quill and the base with a length of metal. The metal loads the float and the protruding section of metal takes the length of rubber by which the float is fastened to the line (*Fig. 10*)

rom a plastic drinking straw. One end is plugged with about half
an inch of peacock quill and a piece of either copper wire or wire nail
s inserted into the base. This wire loads the float, and ideally it
needs only a No. 4 shot placed fifteen inches from the hook to set it
completely. See Fig. 10.

This float is fished from the bottom end only, being fastened by a
single piece of valve rubber which fits conveniently over the protrud-
ng end of the metal insert.

These floats are extremely sensitive but, because they are very slim,
they do tend to pierce the water rather deeply on impact with the
surface after casting. This is not a good thing in very shallow water
out at the same time the float has proved itself very sensitive, competent at beating the drift and easy to cast.

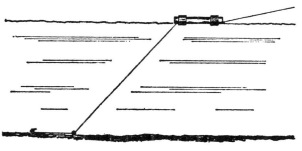

FIG. 11

The peacock-quill float fished flat on the surface

Another float which has served me well is one that has proved very
uccessful for fishing under the rod top on local canals and also on
he River Weaver. This float is simply an inch-long length of thick
peacock quill, fastened to the line with two rubbers.

It takes two No. 8 or one No. 6 shot, depending on the thickness
of the quill. It is fished laying flat on the surface—it doesn't cock like
normal floats. See Fig. 11. I have used it to win contests both on
anals and on the River Weaver. In the River Weaver I fished as
much as five feet over-depth in eight to nine feet of water. I let the
loat drift with the wind until it was held still as the line drew tight
o the rod top. This method brought some above-average size fish,
specially when baiting with caster. Other Weaver anglers quickly
opied the idea and it has continued to be used successfully in recent
ears.

For the faster-flowing rivers I make a bigger version of my stick

float for use when fishing from the near bank to mid-river. The sam
principle of a buoyant tip and a heavy base is useful for taking suc
fish as chub and big roach. The biggest float I have takes the equiva
lent of four AAA—one close under the float, and the others even
spaced through the depth being fished, but with one BB draggir
the bottom.

These heavy stick floats have blunt tips. Greater buoyancy
necessary in rivers like the Severn and Ribble, where the flow
strong. The float must hold up to the surface, resisting the dow
wards pull of turbulent areas of water. These big stick floats run to
maximum of twelve inches in length. There is a fine taper from t
to base, with the balsa being five-sixteenths of an inch thick at tl
tip. See Fig. 12.

Of course, there are limits to the use of these floats. Because th
are so long they should only be used in water at least five feet dee

FIG. 12

The large stick float used for fishing the River Severn.
This is a maximum of twelve inches long and with a
diameter of five-sixteenths inch at the tip. It takes up
to four AAA shot

otherwise the surface disturbance created when the float hits the water after casting scares the fish away.

For fishing the shallower fast-flowing swims that occur up to fifteen yards out from the near bank I stick to cane and balsa floats but use totally different models. I turn to short floats, from five to seven inches long, with all-cane stems but carrying oval-shaped balsa bodies. These have similar shot-carrying capacities to the bigger stick floats and, like the stick floats, are fastened top and bottom to the line. See Fig. 13.

If I want to fish the far side of the River Severn I use an even shorter float, some four inches long and with a cork body. To withstand the pull of the current the float has to be very buoyant and for that reason this one has a peacock quill instead of a cane stem. See Fig. 15. An additional advantage in having a peacock instead of a balsa stem is that the float, while carrying more shot for casting, is not so heavy in itself. Thus it doesn't make so much commotion when it hits the water. Bear in mind that when you cast to the far side of a river like the Severn the water is often shallow over there. It may only be three to four feet deep. Thus the floats must make as little surface impact as possible. Since this float is so very buoyant and short, it is fastened at the base only. This base-only fastening is important in long casting. There is always the tendency for a float to turn over in flight if fastened at each end and when it turns it tangles the terminal tackle. This rarely happens with a float fastened at the base only.

But bearing in mind that these floats are cast long distances it is important to make safeguards to ensure the float is not lost as the result of the base rubber being cut through by the line. It pays to have an eyed ring at the base. The line is passed through the ring just once and then the rubber pushed over the top of it. See Fig. 15.

These big floats are, of course, not designed for catching small fish. No-one casts to the far bank of a river like the Severn for dace and small roach. This is basically a chub float. It takes three swan shot and a single AAA. The three swan are placed close to the float. Two are fastened immediately below the base and rubber and the other is fixed above the base ring. The AAA is positioned fifteen inches from the hook. See Fig. 14.

I prefer to use three swan shot on the line instead of building weight into the float because I can then vary the placing of the shot if I want to. I can also fish with less weight if I think it useful, for, at long distances like this, big fish will pull hard enough to make bites register on under-shotted floats.

When fishing slow-moving bream rivers I never cast the full depth

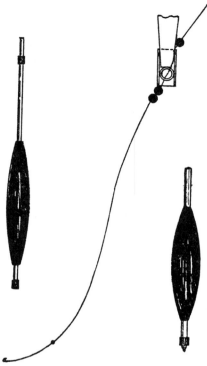

FIG. 13   FIG. 14   FIG. 15

The cane-stemmed and balsa-bodied float used for
shallow, fast-flowing swims up to fifteen yards from the
near bank (*Fig. 13*). How the float in Fig. 14 is fastened
to the line with the aid of valve rubber and a base ring.
Note the position of the three swan shot and the single
AAA shot near the hook (*Fig. 14*). The buoyant peacock-stemmed and cork-bodied float used for long
casting on shallow, fast-flowing rivers (*Fig. 15*)

with a fixed float where there is more than six feet of water. In waters
exceeding that depth I prefer to use a sliding float, even though the
float may only be set to slide a couple of feet. The great advantage is
that the weight of the shot and the float are kept close together
during casting and this is a great aid to accuracy. My rule is never
to have the bulk of the shot used to set the float closer than four feet
to the hook. To put the shot any closer to the hook would inevitably
mean fewer and poorer bites.

This positioning of the shot is of extreme importance. Lots of anglers claim to use the sliding float effectively but some of the queer shotting patterns I have seen in use suggest that many cannot possibly get good results. Shot must not be graduated evenly through the full length of line below the float. The big swan shot must be bunched together and only two very much smaller shot are placed nearer the hook. See Fig. 16. These small shot are both of the same size; whether they are both BB or both No. 4 shot depends on the flow of the water. Spacing the shot evenly along the line leads to tangles during casting. Many precious minutes can be lost in the duration of a contest if this is allowed to happen.

It is possible to use sliding floats carrying from one to four swan shot but the same shotting principle applies. The main shot must always be bunched.

Peacock quill is the natural choice for the stem of sliding floats. This is lighter and doesn't create the pronounced surface impact evident with cane-stemmed floats. In addition the peacock is much more buoyant and therefore holds up to the surface better than cane. Wind and water turbulence cannot brush it aside so easily as can be done to cane. When cast through the air, the peacock-stemmed float doesn't wobble in flight but follows a clean course. This is vital for accurate casting.

Peacock quills are cheap and easy to work with. The long tapered quill gives anglers ample choice when selecting a width and taper suitable for their particular purpose.

But the body and the shape of the body are also very important. There are three materials which can be used to make the bodies. These are elder pith, cork and balsa. My preference is for cork. Cork is really the lightest of the three. At first sight elder pith might seem the lighter material but remember it has to be sealed in order to make it watertight. When this has been done the pith is then as heavy as, if not heavier than, cork. And, unless it is properly seasoned, pith can be very brittle and will fracture easily.

I prefer a long, tapered body to a short fat one. The taper must be even, with the maximum width in the centre. This streamlined body undoubtedly helps casting. In flight these floats move through the air like darts, with a minimum of resistance. See Fig. 17.

Some men prefer to use short fat bodies but these do have a grave disadvantage when the float is required to slide anything more than two feet. Whereas the slim-bodied float remains on the surface in the position to which it has been cast, once the sliding action begins there is the tendency for a dumpy-bodied float to work back towards the angler. This leads to loss of distance before the bait reaches the

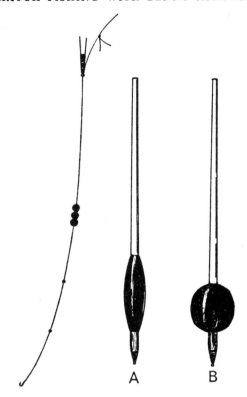

FIG. 16   FIG. 17

The arrangement of the shot when using a sliding float.
The swan shot are bunched together, with two small
shot equidistant between the swan shot and the hook
(*Fig. 16*). The right and wrong bodies for long casting
floats. Drawing (A) shows a streamlined body which
casts smoothly and (B) a body which creates resistance
in flight, thus losing distance and accuracy (*Fig. 17*)

bottom and may mean that the bait is subsequently off the ground
baited patch.

To keep the number of floats in the tackle box to reasonab
proportions I find it useful to have detachable bodies of differer
sizes. This also means that I can change the shot-carrying capaci
of the float without having to break the tackle down. This sav
valuable time. See Fig. 18.

It must be remembered however that the narrower end of the peacock quill must be used as the tip of the float, for otherwise the body cannot be removed, since it cannot be drawn past the base ring. See Fig. 18.

The rings of sliding floats are crucial. They must be made very carefully from soft fine wire. I find fuse wire ideal. The rings are made by turning the wire around the tip of a very fine needle. The wire

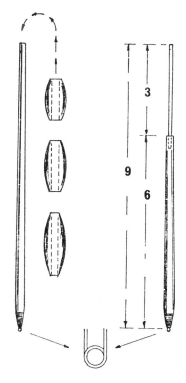

FIG. 18   FIG. 19   FIG. 20

Interchangeable bodies for a peacock-stemmed float. The shot-carrying capacity can be quickly altered during a contest to suit circumstances which can arise because of changing conditions (*Fig. 18*). The exaggerated drawing of the base ring of the sliding float showing a double turn of wire (*Fig. 19*). The two-piece peacock-quill float used for fishing the River Welland (*Fig. 20*)

should be turned to make two complete circles—once is not enough.
See Fig. 19. The double ring is both stronger and finer than the single
circle. It retains its shape better and is not so easily damaged. But
care must be taken to see that the ring is fitted very close indeed to
the end of the base of the float. It should not protrude away from the
float itself.

While there are many bream rivers where my sliding float technique can be applied, rivers like the Witham and the Relief Channel
for example, there are many others where the depth is less than six
feet and where a slider is impracticable. I would place Welbeck
Lakes in this category, for many swims there are less than six feet
deep. Another well-known example is the River Welland.

So, for these relatively shallow waters, I have to use a fixed float.
My floats in this particular range are made from peacock quill and
are simply stems without cork bodies. Instead I have a stem made
from two lengths of quill of differing thicknesses. The base of these
floats is made from a length of thick quill with a thinner inset tip.
The inset is exactly one-third of the overall length of the float. In
other words if the float is nine inches long then the inset is three
inches long. See Fig. 20.

These floats are, of course, much lighter and do not carry so much
shot as do the sliding floats used on deeper water. Their shot-carrying
range varies between three AAA and two No. 4 to three BB and the
two No. 4. Obviously the heavier float is used either for longer
casting or to combat more difficult fishing conditions. But these floats
are not heavy enough for long range work, being impractical at a
greater distance than the middle of the Welland.

When I cast a fixed float the full width of the Welland I use what
is really a cork-bodied slider but use it in a fixed position. It is a
float taking not less than two swan shot and an AAA; anything less
would be incapable of reaching and maintaining distance. I stick to
the inset principle as an aid to casting but now the inset is two-thirds
of the length of the float instead of one-third. See Fig. 21.

I lock a swan shot either side of the base of the float, one above
and one below the ring. Any additional shot is placed below the ring
close to the float—except of course for the single BB which is
positioned eighteen inches from the hook. I have found through
experience that one swan shot is the absolute limit to place above the
ring of the float. That's why any additional shot must be placed
below the float. In that position it aids casting and is also helpful on
the strike. See Fig. 21.

Some men will wonder why I do not use a weighted or zoomer type
of float. I have found weighted floats do not cast either so accurately

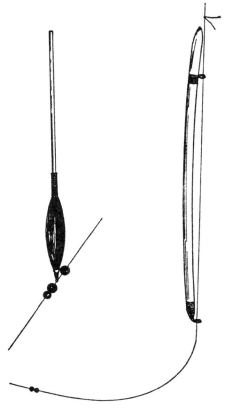

FIG. 21   FIG. 22

The fixed float used for long casting across the River Welland. Notice the float is locked in position by three shot—two swan and one BB. Shot fastened in this position prevent the float penetrating deeply into the water on impact with the surface (*Fig. 21*). The goose-quill sliding float used in flowing water. The base ring is turned outwards and both rings are in line (*Fig. 22*)

or so far as those with the shot nipped on at the base. And loaded floats penetrate the water too deeply on hitting the surface.

The single-ring sliding float can only be used in either still or very slow-moving water. In faster flow the tip of the float drags under the surface and clearly some other method has to be found.

One way out of this problem, where a sliding float is useful in deep and moving water, is to use two rings instead of one. The additional ring is placed an inch from the top of the float.

This float is particularly useful when fishing from banks where casting is obstructed by trees and other bankside vegetation. I have used it on the Severn when the water has been between eight and ten feet deep. But it is not a float to use for long casting. It has a limit of around three rod lengths out, beyond which it is ineffective and might just as well be replaced by the normal swimming-the-stream type of float.

My two-ring slider is made from a goose quill and carries the equivalent of two AAA and one BB shot. The base ring is identical to that on the single-ring slider, but with the exception that it has to be turned outwards so that the line drops straight through it. The top ring is whipped on to the float parallel with the base ring. See Fig. 22. A stop knot is used in the same way as with other sliding floats.

When the flow is light it is possible to use the peacock-stemmed slider but when there is any appreciable flow then the goose quill is far better because of its greater buoyancy. These floats can, of course, be made in smaller sizes, carrying as little as three BB shot.

It must be remembered, however, that this float is for swimming the stream for fish such as roach and chub which are feeding on or close to the bottom. The shotting therefore is very different to that employed on a still water when after bream. Since you will be fishing from a difficult position most casting will be either underhand or sideways. When fishing in nine feet of water I find it best for the float to be set to slide half the depth. The two AAA are bunched together at the lower limit of the distance the float can slide. The remaining BB is fixed eighteen inches from the hook.

Striking at bites can be difficult and can lead to breakages if not carried out with some thought. The action of striking has to be upwards rather than sideways so that the line is drawn up through the float. If the strike is sideways this means that the float itself tends to move upstream against the flow and this puts extreme pressure on the line.

One vital factor is the visibility of float tops. Although there are a wide range of colours available, I prefer to stick to black and white occasionally also using light orange. Half my floats are all-black from the base upwards, others are tipped with white or light orange. I find these simple variations adequate. The black shows up well in white water and the white in black water and shadow. The orange is usually best in narrow waters where water colours conflict and where the learness of the background makes a further complication. On days when fishing at long range in choppy water the orange is better than either black or white since it contrasts with both black and white of the water.

Another point always worth bearing in mind is that floats that are intended for use at long range should be as thick as sensitivity permits at the tip. This helps to eliminate eyestrain. Floats used for near-bank fishing can, of course, be correspondingly finer.

As an aid to bite detection there are coloured plastic float caps which can be used to vary the colour of the float tip on days when the light changes. These can undoubtedly be used to increase visibility but, I find, at the expense of casting. These plastic caps, small as they are, weight the tip and prevent good casting. See Fig. 23.

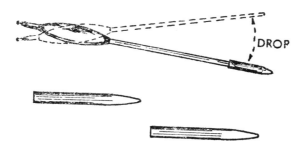

FIG. 23

Plastic float caps and how these weigh down the tip of
the float during casting, making it difficult to achieve
accuracy and distance

There are a number of methods anglers use to stop the sliding float at the required depth. Some men use small split shot, others pieces of valve rubber and even small lengths cut from an elastic band. But I am sure there is nothing better than a nylon stop, made from a length of line the same breaking strain as that being used on the reel.

At one time this stop knot was made by means of a complicated whipping-type knot which is difficult to tie. By experimenting at home for hours on end I finally came across a simple knot which anyone can tie, either at home or at the waterside, in a matter of seconds.

Take a short length of the reel line, about ten inches long. Lay it alongside the reel line close to its required position. This need not be exact for, after all, the knot will slide once it's tied. Make a complete loop, working from one end of the line, and then hold this loop

D

in position on the reel line between finger and thumb. Now take o
end and pass it through the loop and over the reel line three tim
This is sufficient. All that's now needed is to pull the ends tight a
the knot is made. The ends are then trimmed off, but do not ma
the mistake of cutting them off too close to the knot. I find that it
best to leave an inch and a half on each end, clear of the knot. Tl
means that the ends can be pulled to tighten the knot should it slack
off. See Fig. 24.

It can be seen when fishing very deep, thirty feet for instance, tl
the knot will be wound on to the reel before casting. Because of tl
it is essential that the knot should be as small as possible, for oth
wise it will foul the rod rings and impede casting. Another point h
is that if the ends of the stop knot have been cut off close to the kr
the ends stand up on the spool instead of lying flat. If they stand
they upset casting, if they lie down they are perfectly all right.

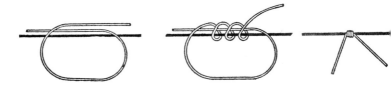

FIG. 24

The simple nylon stop knot used for stopping the
sliding float at the depth to be fished

5. Miscellaneous Tackle

Catapults and Throwing Sticks

NEITHER CATAPULTS NOR throwing sticks are allowed to be used for lose-feeding maggots, casters and groundbait in the National Championship and many big open contests. I have always thought his a very silly ban since both can lead to increased catches of fish. As I see it there is nothing wrong in using a catapult to feed a swim. When a man is able to use a catapult he doesn't need to use the large quantities of groundbait he would otherwise find necessary in order to get his maggots or casters out to a distant swim.

Thus there is less chance of the fish being over-fed and sport is likely to be better for everyone. Sooner or later this silly ban will be lifted but in the meantime the use of both catapults and throwing sticks is restricted to certain areas of the country. They are, for instance, allowed in many northern association matches.

I use a catapult whenever the match rules allow. I find a catapult with a light alloy frame best. This should have prongs set five inches apart, decreasing to four inches above the handle. Each prong should be five inches long and the handle five to six inches long.

I use three-sixteenths inch square elastic, although circular elastic is probably just as good. The length of the two pieces of elastic varies with the size of the man who is to use the catapult. I am 5 ft. 7 in. tall and find lengths of between twelve and fifteen inches about right. In addition there has to be an allowance for the amount required to fasten to the prong and on to the pouch—a further three inches. Care must be taken to see that both lengths of elastic are exactly the same length.

The pouch is made from thin, pliable leather. It measures five inches long by four inches wide, which means that when it is folded its holding capacity is two and a half by four inches. I mitre the corners of the leather with a knife.

Nobody can master a catapult without practice but, eventually, anglers can attain extreme accuracy and are able to hurl a bunch of maggots twenty yards on a windless day. Casters can be sent

51

even further. With a back wind maximum range is around thi
yards. Groundbait can be hurled forty yards.

There is nothing immoral in using catapults. I can think of l
of older anglers who would benefit if these were not banned,
they would be able to compete at swim-feeding with the youngst
who are stronger and can throw their groundbait much further tł
these older fellows.

Many anglers from the Midlands and the southern parts of
country will never have seen a throwing stick. This is a simple deʌ
which I first used in order to project maggots and casters across can
when I was fishing close to the far bank. Obviously I cannot thr
them that far by hand.

The advantage in using one of these sticks is that light feed—eʌ

FIG. 25

The throwing stick used for projecting loose feed—
maggots or casters—long distances, thus eliminating
the need for cereal groundbait to contain the feed

squatts—can be loose-fed across the water without being enclosed in cereal groundbait. This not only reduces the amount of food given to the fish—ensuring that they feed for greater lengths of time—but also eliminates the surface disturbance created when bombs of groundbait hit the water.

My first throwing stick was an adapted bicycle pump. I cut off the adapter end and then inserted a tight-fitting cork plug an inch and three-quarters inside the wall of the pump to act as a stop. See Fig. 25. The maggots or casters—whatever they were—were placed in this cup and, with the handle of the pump extended, the feed flicked out across the water. The feed bunched beautifully and this was to prove one of the reasons why I was able to do so well in canal contests. The more compact the feed the more compact become the shoals of fish.

To ensure that the feed always remains compact, I strongly advise all anglers who make their own throwing sticks to set the cork plug forming the base of the cup that holds the feed at exactly one and three-quarter inches from the tip of the throwing stick. Set at either a greater or lesser distance the plug does not allow the feed to leave the stick at the correct moment—and this leads to inaccurate feeding over a much bigger area of water than is desirable—thus dispersing the fish.

I found the handle of the bicycle pump was not rigid enough and I replaced this with a six inch wooden extension to the pump's casing. See Fig. 25. The throwing stick I use these days is made from a two foot three inch length of light alloy which has an internal diameter of seven-eigths inch. If I want to hurl the feed the maximum distance I grip the stick close to the base—this gives me maximum leverage on the feed placed in the cup at the top of the stick. But if I am fishing a narrow canal, where smaller distances are involved, I then grip the throwing stick as much as twelve inches up from the base.

Shot

The best shot is the softest shot. This is not available in every shop but it is definitely worth going from place to place until the best quality is obtained. I always look for deeply-cut shot, with the vee dead in the centre.

The range of shot I carry in my fishing basket runs from No. 8 shot upwards and includes No. 6, No. 4, BB, AAA and swan shot. I keep all the small shot in separate containers but I do mix the swan and AAA together since I use less of these than of the others —and they are easily distinguishable.

Arlesey Bombs

My range is from a quarter ounce upwards to one ounce. I use more of the half ounce than of the others and have six of these in my box to three of the other sizes. If I run short of one particular size during a day's fishing it is a simple matter to cut some of the lead off one of the bigger bombs. The waters that I fish do not call for any other types of legers.

Plummets

I seldom use a plummet. I have never found a plummet very reliable when trying to assess depth at long range. I find I can gauge depth much quicker and more accurately—without causing so much disturbance—if I watch the reaction of my float when actually fishing. The only time I would consider using a plummet—and this then takes the form of an extra swan shot nipped temporarily on to the line—is when checking the depth in a flowing river when fishing close to the near bank. Plumbing the depth under the rod top can be done much more accurately than when fishing at long range. In this instance—and in this only—I would use a plummet. In my opinion manufacturers' plummets are far too heavy and unwieldy.

Disgorgers

I carry two types of disgorger, relying principally on the button-hook type which is unbeatable for speed. When the hook is in the fish's throat I use the slit barrel type. The vee-type, forked disgorger is very poor and causes too much injury to the fish. It is too haphazard, for unlike the two types already mentioned it does not travel down the line to the hook shank. With the vee type of disgorger the angler has to rely on his own ability to locate the hook, and he is frequently wrong! His probings lead to injured fish. See Fig. 26.

Keepnets

Match anglers must always use large keepnets. Mine is eight feet long, a big net of minnow mesh. This minnow mesh is more expensive but pays for itself over a long period. In canal fishing in particular some of the fish that are caught are often very small. It is an easy matter for these tiny fish to find their way out through bigger mesh. This can easily cost an angler a couple of ounces or so of fish and could make all the difference between winning and being several places down in the prize list.

FIG. 26

Three types of disgorger. (A) is ideal for removing the hook from deeply-hooked fish. (B) is inefficient and causes injury to fish. (C) is very fast when used to remove hooks just inside a fish's mouth

Landing Nets

The standard size net is quite adequate for match fishing but metal extending handles must have regular attention. These handles stick all too often unless they are oiled and greased regularly. When the smaller fish are feeding and there is little chance of anything really big, it pays to knot the net, reducing its depth, so that the fish can be removed more easily. Perhaps the best way of temporarily reducing the length of a landing net is to place a tight rubber band around it. Then, if you hook a big fish and need the full depth of the net, it is easier to remove this than to untie the knot.

Rod Rests

While rod rests are quite standard pieces of equipment these a
sufficiently varied to be either good or bad. It is essential to buy
rest with a wide gape. If the rod has to be laid down hurriedly it ha:
better chance of dropping into the rest if this is a big one. Wi
smaller rests anglers frequently miss the rest altogether and dr
their rod tips into the water. This could be very damaging if fish a
being caught close to the near bank—and, of course, it also wast
time.

With big rod rests there is also less chance of the reel line fouli
on the underside of one arm of the rest. When this happens it is n
uncommon for anglers to smash their lines on the strike. It helps
have two rests when legering. One is positioned to take the mid(
of the rod when the butt is held in the hand but, if the angler wa»
to groundbait and has to lay the butt of the rod down, the angle
the rod in relation to the line is altered. Better to have a rest rea
placed to act as a butt rest for such occasions. There is then a bett
chance of hooking fish that feed when attention is temporar
diverted.

Umbrellas

Only the best and the biggest umbrellas are good enough. Whenev
these are opened and set up they should be pegged to the grour
The wind may be light at the time, but gales spring up quickly and
is better to be safe than sorry. There should always be a strong cc
and peg attached to the umbrella head.

Eye Shields and Sun Glasses

As a personal preference I prefer an eye shade to polarising glass
The shade eliminates both the glare from the sun and the brightn(
of the sky. I am blessed with good eyesight but other anglers m
find glasses helpful.

Clothing

I believe in wearing the minimum amount of clothing when fishi
In the summer I wear a sleeveless tee-shirt so that my arms are
fettered and I have free movement. In the winter, of course, it
better to dress heavily and to be comfortable. But, even so, I try
keep a minimum of clothing on my arms. As long as my body is wa:

and dry my arms largely look after themselves. A good waterproof suit may be useful to some anglers but this can be cumbersome and I like to manage without, relying on my umbrellas to keep me dry. I do, however, wear waterproof over-trousers. When fishing rivers like the Trent, where the banks are good and I don't have to walk far, I wear fur-lined boots, but when the bank is wet and marshy then I wear rubber boots. One point here. Find yourself the lightest pair of rubber boots you can get. The three-quarter length are ideal, for the reduction in weight means a saving in energy.

Bite Indicators

I use a home-made butt-bite indicator for still-water bream fishing. The indicator arm is made from an eight inch length of peacock quill and I never put weight on it. In fact, the lighter it is the better. Mine is simply this length of quill and a rubber connecting link to a Terry clip. I fasten the clip on to the upper whipping of the lower ring on the middle joint. The end ring of the indicator is a simple double circle of copper wire whipped into position. The materials cost fourpence at the most. See plate eight.

Of course this butt-bite indicator is useless in flowing water and I use a swingtip. I have already mentioned that I prefer to weight the tip to counter-act the lifting effect of flowing water. I use no more lead than is absolutely necessary, and prefer to manage without it if at all possible.

6. Maggots and Casters

Maggots and Casters

QUALITY OF BAIT is without question the greatest single contributory factor to a match angler's success. I believe this has been widely accepted in the last few years and hundreds of men go to enormous trouble to see that when match day comes around they are equipped with the finest hook and feeder maggots it is possible to obtain.

I have always been very conscious of the value of tip-top maggots and it was largely my success in breeding good-quality feed in my early days as a match angler that finally prompted me to become a professional breeder.

As many as thirty years ago there were numbers of star anglers who bred their own maggots in the Leigh area of Lancashire. The bait they bred would still be top quality by today's standards. They produced gozzers thirty years ago, they were the first to find the way to produce squatts on a large scale, they bred the deadly bran and sour milk maggots, they perfected the anatto maggot and also experimented to produce such by-products as the anattoed pinkie (sometimes known as the anatto runner).

They were extremely knowledgeable men and knew the difference between a good fly and an inferior one. They knew the correct feeding methods to ensure that maggots reached full maturity and were able to make the very best possible use of their limited resources.

I consider myself to have been more than lucky to have learned from many of these anglers. They taught me a very great deal about maggot breeding, much of which is still 'secret' today. The time spent obtaining top-quality maggots is never wasted. It is a demanding pastime but pays for itself with improved catches of fish.

Large commercial maggots

The large commercial maggot, the one available in all tackle shops, has come in for a great deal of criticism and special hook maggots have been produced with the intention of obtaining something much better. The good commercial maggot comes from one of the two common British bluebottles, *Calliphora vomitoria*. The other bluebottle common in this country, *Calliphora erythrocephala*, is the fly which produces the gozzer maggot. But commercial maggots will always produce bites in all well-stocked waters and even in others on days when fish are feeding well.

These maggots are easy to produce and do not require specialist feeding. They can be bred in huge quantities to meet the mass market and are fed on what would otherwise be waste material—condemned meat and fish. They are not so vulnerable to misuse as specials, and can be kept longer and will travel better. They can be sent long distances by rail in gallon tins and do not suffer undue deterioration as the result.

This cannot be said for specials. Some men breed gozzers on such expensive food as partridges and pheasants. From this it can be clearly seen that special maggots are expensive and the average angler would have to pay as much as one pound a pint for them. Clearly they would be an impractical commercial proposition.

The average angler still doesn't really know the difference between one hook maggot and the next. He is satisfied with his shop-bought commercial maggots and can catch fish on them; particularly when he fishes on his own, away from the exacting demands of match fishing.

The special maggot, the superior bait, comes into its own when fish are feeding shyly and when the extra fish or two is needed to win a contest. But there will always be a big demand for commercial maggots and this demand has even increased in recent years since it was discovered that these maggots, properly handled, produce the best-quality casters.

Giving value for money, they can be used freely for loose feeding. They can be colour-fed or dyed to a variety of colours which may appeal to fish under the different conditions. The size of these maggots varies from breeder to breeder but all commercial maggots have the potential to reach the same size. The smaller ones are those which have been taken away from their feed before they are fully developed.

Provided the bait has been produced from the right fly there is no real merit in super-large maggots. The great mass of anglers have always assumed the biggest to be the best, but this is not necessarily the case. There are days when fish—whether they are roach or bream—will take a small maggot in preference to a big one. But it is right to say that maggots that have reached maximum size are more likely to be good ones. They have reached maximum development, the smaller ones have not.

In commercial maggot farms the breeder almost always tries to increase output beyond what his premises are really capable of providing. Thus he often has too many maggots growing up together and the result is competition for food. This sometimes means there is not enough food for them all. They take longer to reach maturity and because of this have tougher skins than is desirable. The tougher the skin the more likely a fish is to reject the maggot.

Some maggots are packed in very rough sawdust before despatch to tackle shops. Sawdust is really the best agent in which to pack maggots during the delivery stage, when they are fresh off the meat and need some scouring to remove surplus grease and moisure. In this early stage the maggots excrete moisture. They clean themselves and, as they do, tend to lose some of their size. Fine, clean sawdust should always be used.

There is no alternative to sawdust. If fresh maggots are put into either bread or bran in any quantity they create heat, and this in turn makes them active, sweat, and diminish in size. The maggot works frantically under these conditions but when transferred to clean bran or dry breadcrumb seems to lose its energy and strength

So the tackle dealer always receives his maggots from the breeder packed in sawdust. But many dealers know that this sawdust should be riddled off and be replaced either by bran or fine bread—once the maggots have passed through the cleaning stage. More and more tackle dealers are putting their maggots into bran or bread before selling them to anglers. But once an angler buys his maggots from the shop they still require quite a lot of treatment to ensure they are in the best possible condition.

Whether the maggots are bought in sawdust, bran or fine bread they should be riddled right away. They should then be placed in clean, dry bran overnight. Then next morning they should be riddled again and the bran replaced with the finest of fine bread which has been slightly dampened. This ensures that the maggots have no smell whatsoever and that they are perfectly clean. This last-minute dampening is designed to moisten the maggots with the object of keeping their skins soft.

This may seem to be a lot of trouble, but the knowledge that comes with having bait in top condition also gives satisfaction and confidence, as well as the chance of an improved catch.

There are many times when coloured maggots are better than the natural ones. But my own preference is limited to anatto (light orange) and plain white. Just occasionally I will use canary yellow or maggots coloured a pale shade of pink. But a most important point is that the maggots must be colour-fed and not simply dyed

In other words, the colouring matter is put on to the food the maggots eat rather than on to the maggots themselves once they have reached maturity.

There are lots of anglers who use chrysodine-dyed maggots, but this is harmful. This dye burns the skin of the maggot and takes away its liveliness. Thus when it is placed on the hook the maggot is never so effective as one which has been colour-fed. I therefore strongly advise anglers who do not breed their own to buy maggots which have been coloured by the breeder.

During warm weather maggots can be kept most successfully in a refrigerator but they should never be deep-frozen. They should never be chilled to the stage when they go completely dormant but should be allowed to retain a limited amount of life and movement. However, there is a limit to the time it is wise to keep hook maggots in a fridge. I find this time limit to be about four days. Thus maggots left from one weekend's fishing cannot be placed in the fridge and used the following weekend as hookbait. They would in most cases only be good enough for feed.

To ensure that their maggots are of top quality each breeder takes special care with his chrysalids which are to be the breeding stock for future production. These chrysalids—or casters as they are now called—are carefully sorted and any deformed or blackened casters taken away and destroyed. Thus the breeder is able to carry on production with flies of the same species and this leads to maggots of a uniform size and quality.

When the casters are allowed to hatch out they produce large black dull-looking bluebottles—*Calliphora vomitoria*.

These produce far better maggots than the shiny black flies, *Phormia terra novae*. These shiny blacks produce useless maggots, very slow-moving and hard-skinned. Reputable breeders try to eliminate these flies from their fly houses.

Casters

In 1953 I started experimenting to see what results I could obtain in attempting to produce sinking casters which could be used as loose feed for roach fishing, but I was fully committed to producing maggots for sale and hadn't really the time to concentrate my efforts. Thus the development of caster fishing took several years.

I had first thought casters would make a first-class bait when noting the wonderful appearance and attractiveness of the casters I had on the maggot farm for breeding purposes. At that time I had a partner in the business, Alf Pendlebury, who was not a particularly skilful angler. I suggested to Alf that he try these casters and since we were breeding large quantities of maggots it was easy to obtain a couple of pints of sinking casters from the gallons that were in stock. Alf could never do well when maggot fishing, but baiting with casters he achieved such success that he became a fanatic with them. He spent lots of time—and finally so did I—using casters, and we found there were many days when we could catch fish that would not look at a maggot.

Casters are full of protein. That much I was sure of even before I first began to experiment to produce the sinking casters that were subsequently to have great success with Trent roach. I had supplied lots to a miller who had experimented by feeding them to chickens, mixed in with their normal food. The chickens that were fed casters grew plumper and reached maturity sooner than those given only normal poultry food. What's more, the birds that were fed casters picked these out of the food. They developed a preoccupation for them.

I developed the sinking caster and first put it to use on Lancashire canals and in the River Weaver in 1956. That was a wonderful season for me. During that time I won eight big open matches, five association matches and something like a score of sweepstakes. I broke the match-weight record for the Weaver with a catch of 17 lb. in a four-hour match, and did the same on the Leeds and Liverpool Canal at Leigh with an 8 lb. 5 oz. catch of roach. In addition I cracked the Wigan Centre record for a two-hour contest in their Adlington Canal with 5 lb. 11 oz.

Small wonder I had every confidence in them when I first took casters to the Trent. The very first time I used them was a fifty-a-side Manchester versus Nottingham contest. I won with just under 17 lb. in three and a half hours and the next man had 12 lb. But casters have their limitations. I have found they are no use in coloured water. They have failed many times on the Calder under these conditions and at such times I am sure the anatto maggot is far superior.

But I have caught bream on casters. I have taken a 60 lb. catch from the Warrington Canal on them. Some of the catch that day were good perch and there were also some good-quality roach, but the bulk of the total was bream. The biggest bream was a three-pounder and, with three exceptions, the bream were all in the 1 lb. to 2¼ lb. range.

I have tried casters for bream on both the Witham and the Welland without success. But these experiments were made at a time when bream were not being caught on maggot either and I cannot yet dismiss them as failures on those rivers.

I have found casters to be a remarkable bait for roach in any water. They can be a bit dodgy in the early part of the season when the water is warm, but once August has passed I believe they are almost unbeatable. In waters where there is a large number of really big roach I believe that roach catches made by anglers baiting with casters are quite capable of beating the catches made by bream anglers. I particularly fancy the Ten Mile Bank stretch of the Great Ouse for this. And I am equally certain that they will work like a dream on the Hampshire Avon.

Casters also proved themselves on the Severn for chub. Using as many as three on hooks up to size 12, my son Kevin won the Russell Memorial match just below Bridgenorth with 23 lb. of chub in the summer of 1967 in a contest fished by 300 crack matchmen.

There are occasions when casters are not so effective, but I have found that by alternating the bait between these and anatto maggots I have kept the fish feeding. Oddly enough there have been instances where I have fed the swim with casters all through the day and yet took fish on anatto maggots.

Casters are sweeping the board under favourable conditions in the Yorkshire rivers, and I am sure they will eventually be the dominant bait for roach in most of the rivers and still-waters of the country. It doesn't matter whether the rivers are slow or fast, shallow or deep. As long as they are reasonably clear the roach will take casters.

The great point in favour of casters from the angler's viewpoint is that they are relatively cheap. They are much cheaper than maggots—not pint for pint, but fewer are needed for a day's fishing. And it is usually unnecessary to use groundbait with them. On the few occasions when the casters have to be sunk extra quickly because of the high rate of flow groundbait must, of course, be used, but never in any huge quantity.

The first essential in obtaining sinking casters is good-quality maggots that come from the big bluebottle. The maggots have to be fully grown and I feed mine on fish and poultry. They do not have to be fed on meat and certainly not on liver, which anyway is increasingly difficult to obtain.

Having obtained a gallon of the right maggots, anglers who want to develop them to sinking casters can do so with an absolute minimum of waste. There's really no waste at all. The actual preparation takes a week, for under normal conditions it takes a fresh maggot six days to cast. The seventh day, Sunday, is match day and by that time the maggots should be at the caster stage.

The gallon of maggots must first be divided into four equal portions and placed in clean plastic containers. The object in splitting the maggots is to ensure that they are all at exactly the same temperature. Maggots generate heat and the more they are divided the more constant the temperature for all of them.

Cleanliness is of the utmost importance. That's why I prefer plastic containers to tin. Plastic is easier to keep clean. For the first two days the maggots are kept in very fine sawdust. This must have no large wood chips or sticks in it or the maggots will not be properly cleaned.

When the two days have passed, the maggots must be riddled and particular care taken to ensure that no dead maggots remain in with the live ones. These would taint the remainder and prevent them becoming a first-class bait. The maggots are left in more fine, fresh sawdust for a further two days. When this time has elapsed—the end of the fourth day—a close watch must be kept to see if any have begun to cast.

If all is well it is unlikely that any have. Riddle them again and put them back into more fresh, fine sawdust but dampen it slightly with water. The object of the moisture is to smooth the skins of the maggots as they begin to cast and thus to obtain a more attractive bait.

At the end of the fifth day comes the all-important stage. Some maggots will undoubtedly have turned if the temperature has been averaging sixty degrees Fahrenheit. The maggots are again passed through a riddle. The active ones crawl through the gauze but the casters are left behind. At this stage—the end of the fifth day—there will probably be just over half a pint of white and reddening casters. These are placed in a plastic bucket and covered with cold water. They must be kept cool—preferably on a cold concrete floor—but must never be frozen.

On the morning of the sixth day there is fifteen minutes' work that must be done. Of the seven and a half pints of maggots that remain a further two pints should have turned to casters. These are removed by riddling and are then placed in the bucket with the half-pint collected earlier. There's no need whatsoever to change the water.

At this stage two and a half pints of casters are in hand and five and a half pints of maggots remain. Now is the time to force the pace a little by raising the temperature of the maggots a few degrees. They must not be exposed to too much heat but, with a little more warmth, the rate of casting will increase. This eliminates waste.

By the end of the sixth day—Saturday—there should be a further three pints of casters to remove by riddling. These are then placed in the same bucket and the same water as the two and a half pint

Master match angler Benny Ashurst, winner of over 300 contests and widely acknowledged as the country's top match-fishing brain.

2 *Benny Ashurst was well known as a successful canal angler even before the last war. He is pictured in action on the Leigh Canal.*

3　*Part of the Benny Ashurst collection of cups and trophies.*

4 *Horace Storey of the Nottingham Anglers' Association has every reason to smile. He is pictured with his trophies and medals after winning the National Championship on the River Severn in 1957. The river was badly swollen by flood water, and Horace won with 7 lb. 12 oz. 2 dr.*

5 *Jack Thorndike of* Angling Times *upends a bottle of champagne into one of the trophies won by Boston angler Roy Jarvis in the 1966 National Championship.*

5 *Benny Ashurst, Captain of the Stoke City and District Angling Association, draws his team's peg number from Major Brian Halliday.*

7 The camera peeps into Benny Ashurst's float box. His stick floats are fixed inside the lid by a length of elastic. Nothing gaudy here but every float has been designed for a specific purpose.

8 A home-made bite-indicator.

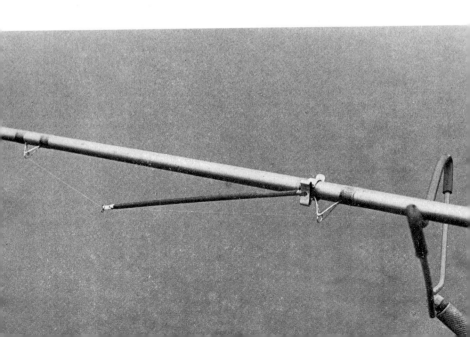

17   *Trotting the stream with a fixed-spool reel. The bale arm of the reel is open and the line is retained on the spool with the forefinger. Line is released as required by simply raising the finger.*

18　Benny has a net of roach and perch to show for a day's fishing in a lake in the East Midlands.

19   Kevin Ashurst, famous son of famous father, nets himself a 1 lb. perch. He is already acknowledged to be one of Britain's top match anglers.

20 *Benny Ashurst swings a River Dee roach into his hand and grabs it first time.*

21 *Benny nets a 3 lb. common carp. The fish took a single caster offered on a size 18 hook.*

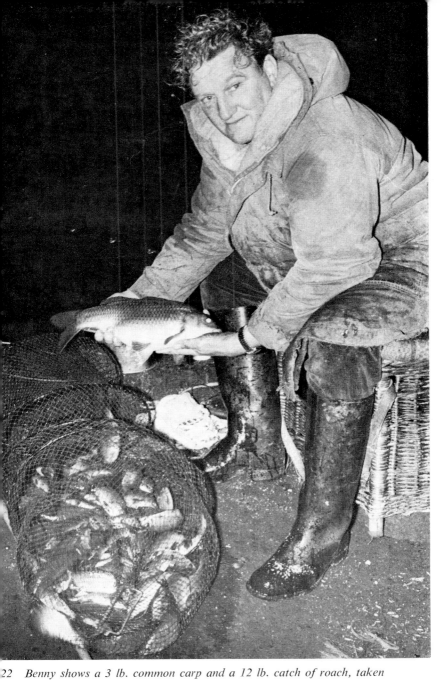

22 *Benny shows a 3 lb. common carp and a 12 lb. catch of roach, taken from the St. Helens Canal, Lancs.*

23 Roach of this size are ideal for building up big contest weights on match rivers. This 6 oz. fish was taken from the swim very quickly and with a minimum of fuss.

already collected. This leaves two and a half pints that have not yet turned.

Last thing on Saturday night remove the casters from the water and place them in a clean but very wet towel. This forces the white casters to redden quickly, while the dampness of the towel ensures they do not turn into floaters, or 'sailors' as I call them.

On the next morning—match day—there might be one or two floaters in the towel. Drop them all into water and, naturally enough, if there are any they will rise to the surface. Skim them off and reject them. If you have been preparing the bait properly there should be no more than a dozen or so. Now put the five and a half pints of casters into your tackle basket, but in a plastic container in which they are just covered with water. This retards further progress and ensures they remain sinkers.

There are, of course, still two and a half pints of maggots that had not turned to casters by Saturday evening. Many of these will have turned by Sunday morning but don't spend any more time on them. Just put them in a container and take them to the match as they are. During the journey to wherever you are fishing more will continue to turn into casters. They are the reserve bait. They are not ready for immediate use. First use the casters that have already been prepared. When these are all gone then use the remainder. All will then be casters, with very few exceptions.

All will be sinkers for they have only just cast. If there are still a few maggots left that's nothing to worry about. They can be fed into the swim mixed with casters and won't do any harm at all. Thus the whole gallon will have been used and should have provided three men with enough hookbait and feed for a five-hour match—on the Trent or a similar river.

There is no special preparation for the casters that are used on the hook. Personally I prefer to pick out a couple of hundred of the dumpiest, for these are the best shape for putting on the hook. They are laid on a damp cloth during the contest. At the end of the match pop the remaining casters back into water. They will keep fresh for a further three days but after that will be useless and must be thrown away. The casters die and ferment. The juices within the shell turn sour. Fish will never take them and it is time wasted to attempt to use them.

As an alternative method the casters can be kept dry in a fridge instead of in water. But they must be kept away from the deep freeze. If they become frozen they are useless.

If the maggots cost one pound a gallon that only works out at six shillings and eightpence a man for bait for five hours' fishing.

E

That's not expensive, especially since some anglers have suggested it takes a gallon of maggots to produce two pints of sinking casters. Try it my way.

The crucial factor in producing a sinking caster is to ensure that the shell remains moist. While the shell contains a quantity of water it will sink. But when it is exposed to the air and conditions under which this moisture evaporates then the shell becomes drier and drier until eventually it no longer sinks. It then floats and is, of course, useless as loose feed.

It is very likely that further development will lead to an era when casters from such small maggots as pinkies and squatts are used for the most delicate types of fishing. Both could probably be applied to canal fishing, where the fish are already shy and where their appetites are much less pronounced than on fast, streamy rivers like the Trent.

Gozzers

Although anglers imagine that gozzers—or dumpies, as we called them thirty years ago—are basically maggots best suited to catching bream, they are equally good for roach fishing. These are not so big as large liver-fed maggots, coming from a bluebottle with the Latin name *Calliphora erythrocephala*.

It is difficult to define why these maggots should be so very attractive to fish, but their main quality seems to be that they are exceptionally soft. Thus once a fish mouths a gozzer it is much more likely to take it than eject it—as it might well do with a commercial maggot.

I should, however, make it clear that I am not particularly fanatical in demanding gozzers for my own fishing, whether in matches or as an individual. I have always done well with my own commercial maggots and I am convinced that a man who draws a peg with a shoal of bream in front of him will catch them just as well on the ordinary hook maggots as anything else. Of course much depends on the method being used and the skill of the individual, but gozzers can never be considered the one factor above all else that decides whether or not bream were caught.

But the use of gozzers does create confidence in the minds of anglers who think they have the very best bait and this does help. In addition, it is not a bad thing to use a different hook maggot to anglers pegged nearby, since fish will often show a fancy for different bait. And, as I have already said, fish will in any case mouth a gozzer that little bit longer than harder-skinned maggots.

Years ago, before I took up breeding maggots commercially, I always used to breed myself a few anatto hook maggots most weeks. I did it in such a way that there wasn't any smell, and the method was completely without annoyance to the neighbours. I used to breed about 100 or so maggots that would last through most contests and they were always of absolute peak quality.

This is what I did: Let us assume it is Friday and you are fishing a contest in eight days' time. Buy a pig's heart from the butcher. This is the ideal amount of feed for the few specials. If you want some white and some anattoes then buy two hearts. You could use sheep's hearts but these are small and you need double the quantity for the same amount of gozzers. You could also use pigeons or chickens but I prefer a heart, since it is the ideal shape. In my view liver is out. This has too much blood in it and the resulting maggots are too dirty. They have the black food spot in them and I do not want this. I prefer my bait to look absolutely clean.

Bearing in mind that you want no smell, if the heart is fresh pop it into the oven for three or four minutes—no more. This dries up the meat, but gives it a slight odour that flies find attractive. Place the heart on a saucer, or something similar, and take it outside to a quiet spot in the garden where there may be a fly or two.

Now comes the crucial part. If you do not take care now you might as well not bother at all! You want blows from the right sort of fly. You do not want greenflies or the big flies that I call 'shiny blacks'. So watch the heart until the right fly has blown it twice. Twice is enough. I used to keep a long cane in my hand and if the wrong flies tried to blow I tapped them away. Two blows are ample. If you get any more there will not be enough feed on the one heart for the maggots to grow to full size, and no matter how you try you cannot scrape blow off once it is on.

You must watch this operation closely. It is useless to put the heart outside and then dash off to a football match. You get too many blows and finish up with lots of tiny maggots with differing parents. It usually takes about forty-five minutes to get the blows. Having got the right blows, bring the heart into a corner of the garage, or a quiet spot, and place it in a one-foot deep bowl which has four inches of clean bran spread over its bottom.

You must nestle the heart into the bran; do not cover it. But before you leave the heart you make three cuts along the length of it. Do not cut right through the meat, but leave hinges of flesh that have not been severed. Bind the cuts back together loosely with wool. Now cover the top of the bowl with thick brown paper and tie it on tightly. Muslin will not do. Flies will blow on the muslin

and the eggs will fall through on to the heart. All this should hav
been completed by Saturday morning at the latest. Now put the bow
out of the way and leave things to run their course.

After twenty-four hours the gozzers will come alive and o
Monday will start to feed. You must have a look at them on Tuesday
At this stage they could be quarter-grown. If they are no bigger all i
well. Leave them until Wednesday. On Wednesday they should b
feeding-mad. This is the time to use the anatto—but first a few word
about anatto itself.

This is difficult to obtain and there are several second-rate sub
stitutes on the market. Genuine anatto is far superior. It comes i
four-ounce rolls which cost about four shillings. Cut a quarter of th
roll off and immerse it in boiling water. An old flask cup makes
perfect container. Cover the anatto by a quarter of an inch. The hea
melts the anatto roll and by stirring you can make it into a thic
but runny liquid like thick paint. It may require a degree c
thinning.

Undo the wool around the heart and paste the anatto thickl
inside the cuts you have already made. Wrap the wool around agai
but do it lightly and do not knot. Then smear the remaining anatt
over the outside of the heart. The heart must not be tied, or the ma
gots will be forced out of the meat prematurely and will not grow.
you want some white gozzers you will, of course, have had tw
hearts blown and you will not anatto the second one.

The stage at which you use the anatto is vital. Do not anatto to
soon or you will stop the little maggots from feeding. They do no
eat anatto because they like it. When they do, it is because they a
madly hungry and eat on in spite of it.

On Thursday the maggots will be three-quarters grown and o
Friday will have fed-up and have begun to leave the remnants of th
heart. They will be cleaning themselves in the bran. Remove th
remainder of the heart, giving it a good shake to eject the remainin
maggots. Burn what is left of the heart. This will be no more than th
outer casing.

Leave the maggots to clean in the bran until Saturday and the
take them out and put them into a slightly-dampened fine ground
bait. There are your maggots all ready for the hook. You will no
buy better in any tackle shop and they are as good as those I us
myself.

Anatto roll will keep indefinitely. It is quite soft when fresh bu
after a while will set almost as hard as concrete. It will not deteriorat
Even when it is bone-hard it will quickly melt once immersed i
boiling water. It is reddish-brown in appearance and the rolls I us

are about an inch and a half in diameter and some four inches long. Each roll will colour-feed four pigs' hearts, so for a full season you will need nine or ten rolls.

Other anglers have suggested that the gozzer comes from a special fly which will only breed in darkness. It has been said that the feed—whether it is sheep's or pigs' hearts or from whole pigeons— must be kept in a dark place with only a tiny apperture of light through which the flies get to the feed. This is not so. Men who breed gozzers in this way have the use of a shed or garage in which they scatter numbers of the gozzer chrysalids. When these hatch out in isolation from other flies, they find the feed laid out for them and naturally enough drop their eggs on to it. Thus every blow results in gozzer maggots.

Flies that do not produce gozzers will not stay in a dark place. They search around until they find a way of escape and lay their eggs in daylight.

Some breeders use sugar with the object of producing gozzers that are not only a degree bigger but are also that little bit softer. Brown demarara sugar is spread over the meat once the maggots have become active and are feeding. The juices in the meat soften and liquefy the sugar. The gozzers then eat a quantity of sugar with the meat.

Gozzers need never be placed in sawdust. This applies to all home-bred maggots. They go straight into bran and are ready for use almost immediately. They do not have to be exposed to such a lengthy cleaning process as commercial maggots.

Gozzers do not have so long an active life as commercial maggots. They very soon clean themselves and turn to chrysalids. Therefore it is necessary to be very careful when planning ahead so that they are in peak condition on the day they are used. Gozzers can be kept in a fridge for short periods thus extending their life cycle.

But gozzers are no recipe for instant success. One of the drawbacks is that they cannot be easily produced in really large numbers and for that reason few men have sufficient to use as feed as well as hookbait. Obviously their effectiveness is increased considerably if the fish can be given some gozzers in the groundbait, for this leads to their taking those on the hook.

Strictly, it pays to have gozzers in anatto and white, and even in pale pink at times. It has been said that white gozzers are best for bream and anatto best for roach, but it is wrong to generalise in this way. In fact there are times when fish have a preference for either colour and they certainly have no fixed ideas. The angler has to discover for himself which is best on the day.

Sour bran specials

Some matchmen produce special hook maggots using sour milk and bran rather than meat. This method eliminates all smell yet produces a hook maggot which in my opinion is even better than the gozzer as a bait for roach. It is difficult to anatto these maggots and, in any case, since they are bred on milk the maggots are so beautifully white this is their prime attraction.

I fill a one pound glass jam jar with bran and then dampen it with water as though I were making a groundbait. I then add enough milk to make this into a wet, but not too sloppy, mixture. I stir it thoroughly with a stick so that the goodness of the milk is absorbed into the bran, thus making it a fattening food.

When this has been completed, the jar is placed in a dark shed and left for a week. In that time the milk goes sour and a crust forms. There are crevices in the crust and, once the milk has soured, the fly, three times bigger than the ordinary housefly, lays its eggs. Although I have produced maggots by this process hundreds of times, I have yet to see a fly actually in the process of laying its eggs. But the advantage of using a clear glass jar is that it is possible to look at the bran from the outside without disturbing the maggots and putting them off feeding.

This is a very slow process and it takes a fortnight from the time the bran is first mixed with the milk until the maggots are ready for use. It is impossible to produce large numbers of maggots by this means. To ensure a steady supply—and have them at the right time—it is necessary to put down one jam jar each day.

When the maggots are quarter-grown I add a dessertspoonful of solid sour milk. I place this in the centre of the jar in a hole made with a small stick. This provides the extra feed needed to enable the maggots to grow to the best possible size. When they have finally finished feeding they look very similar to, and are about the same size as, a gozzer. But they can easily be distinguished from the gozzer since their vent ends are flat and the 'eyes' are very black—more so than on any other maggot. An additional difference is that whereas all other maggots move tapered end first, specials move blunt end first.

It is essential to breed these maggots in a narrow jar rather than something with a wide top since a narrow neck retains the moisture and prevents the bran from drying out.

These specials have a very short life cycle and are turned to chrysalids in as little as two days from the time they have finished feeding.

The easiest way to separate the specials from the bran is to use a small sieve bottomed with zinc gauze similar to that used in the old-fashioned type of meat safe. The bran containing the specials is tipped into the sieve and then placed under a fast-running tap. The water quickly washes away the bran, leaving the specials on the bottom of the sieve. All that's needed then is to add a handful of dry bran and to tip the bran and maggots into the bait tin. They are ready for immediate use.

Pinkies

Pinkies have come into wide use as feeder maggots, mainly on bream rivers, but more often than not they are used by men unable to obtain a regular supply of squatts. But the pinkie is not an inferior maggot. It is a very small but heavy maggot which sinks quickly and is therefore extremely useful in some circumstances.

It comes from the greenbottle, *Lucilia sericata*, and in the first instance was bred more by accident than design. When I first started breeding commercially I had no fly house on my maggot farm. I used to get the feed blown out in the open air and, as a result, a variety of different species of flies laid their eggs on the meat.

When I brought this blown meat inside and placed it in the breeding vat, the pinkies would always be the very first maggots to feed-up. They do this very quickly, taking only four days from blow to attaining full size. They proved to be a very great nuisance.

There was no big demand for them at that time and they increased in numbers so rapidly that they reached the stage when they made it impossible for me to get the meat blown out in the open air. Pinkies are extremely active maggots. They cannot be contained in open-topped tins or vats and will crawl out of almost anything.

As the result of reaching maturity quicker than the other maggots, they used to crawl out of the vat and over the floor of the breeding shed. Although I could anticipate this and collect large numbers of them from the edges of the vat just prior to the time when they were preparing to leave, many got on to the floor and a large proportion escaped from the building altogether. That's why we gave them their first name of 'runners'—the name pinkie came later.

My breeding operations rapidly increased the numbers of greenbottles in the area and this proved a vicious circle. The more maggots I bred the more greenflies I got and in the end I had to build my own fly house in order to exclude them completely.

At that time they were no more than a nuisance. Very few anglers were prepared to buy pinkies. This was eighteen years ago, at a time when match fishing on a national scale was very much more concentrated on roach fishing than it is today. At that time anglers didn't want so much feed as they do now.

However, I used to look at those pinkies and think what effective baits they might be. In fact I took to using them regularly both on the hook and as feed. I used them during the Walker Cup match on the Haigh Canal at Adlington some fourteen years ago and won hands down with a weight of 3 lb. 3 oz. The runner-up had 1 lb. 9 oz. This was followed by wins in a number of local sweepstakes.

Pinkies soon showed they were valuable since they would keep for many weeks, even in the summer. When they were fresh off the meat they were white in colour, but after being off for four days they gradually changed colour to a very pale pink—hence the name pinkie.

Up to this time I used only the pinkies bred by accident. I decided that I would try to get an improved quality since I had done so well with them. But there were special problems here. Greenbottles are flies that revel in heat and, while they are prepared to lay eggs with gusto in the warm sunshine, are inactive on colder days.

I never went to the trouble of making a special fly house for pinkies since I didn't want enough to warrant this. I only wanted a mere handful of improved maggots for the hook. I overcame the difficulty by using the same method as for breeding gozzers, only this time, instead of rejecting the greenbottle, I wanted it to the exclusion of all others. I had to watch while the blow was made and had to tap off all the unwanted flies as soon as they settled.

I anattoed the hearts in the same way as for other anatto maggots and produced an anattoed pinkie, known widely in Lancashire and Cheshire as the anatto runner.

This proved an excellent bait for canal fishing in particular. I won the Walker Cup match at Adlington again the next year with these anatto runners with 2 lb. 15 oz. to the runner-up's 2 lb. 6 oz. I also won matches in the Weaver, the Stafford Open and the A.C.A. Open on the Shropshire Union Canal at Christleton with 6 lb. of small bream.

I had thought that pinkies would be a good hookbait and this view was further reinforced when I topped the 800 competitors in the Manchester Evening Chronicle (now the Manchester Evening News) Open event on the Macclesfield Canal. That win brought me my first-ever gold medal and, as I had promised years before, I gave it to Wilf Dyson, the man who had done so much to encourage me at the start.

I used pinkies as my hookbait in all Lancashire and Cheshire matches until the time when I developed casters and turned over to them exclusively. This, of course, was twelve years ago, and at that time I still hadn't begun to travel far and wide about the country.

I don't think that even the best of the anatto runners—pinkies, if you like—compare with casters, and I have never used them since. If I want hook maggots these days I use either the gozzer, the special, or the plain commercial maggot.

I can appreciate that some anglers can still find a good use for pinkies as feeder maggots. Being heavier than squatts, they are better in flowing rivers as loose feed and, in situations where the large hook maggots are too big to consider using, pinkies have further use.

But I see no point in mixing pinkies and squatts together in the same groundbait, or of using both these feeders in the same swim. My main objection to pinkies as loose feed is that they are lively—even under water. They keep alive for days under water but soon burrow into the soft mud on the bed of a water and are lost from the fishes' view. Squatts, on the other hand, soon drown and lie still on the bottom where they are easily seen and picked up by fish.

Pinkies are also extremely strong. They cannot be compressed so effectively as squatts. When they are used in groundbait there is a very definite limit to the number that can be thrown in any one ball. Unlike squatts they remain active inside the ball of groundbait and can split a ball in mid-air. This in turn leads to inaccurate feeding and consequently to a splitting up of the shoal of fish. One half of the ball of groundbait goes one way and the other half another. The shoal divides and there are fewer fish left in the swim.

Anglers must always remember that if they keep pinkies at home they must use tins with tight-fitting lids. If a lid is not used the pinkies will all crawl out of the tin during the hours of darkness. This even applies if the pinkies are bone-dry.

Squatts

Squatts are the frailest of all the maggots. They are as long as, but very much thinner than, a pinkie and weigh much less. They are the most devastating of all the feeder maggots and are particularly effective for bream fishing, and even for very small fish. They are a hook maggot of no mean ability, particularly on days when fish are finicky. Every species of bottom-feeding fish has a keen eye for squatts. I have won matches on the Bridgewater Canal, both at Warrington and Runcorn, with perch taken on squatts.

The squatt comes from the common housefly, but it is virtually impossible for anglers to breed these for themselves. The difficulty lies in the fact that squatts need a lot of heat and this would be too expensive when producing small quantities. In addition, the housefly is so very small that the flies have to be caged effectively or they will be a nuisance in the neighbourhood. Squatts are nothing like so productive as pinkies. Large numbers of mature flies are needed for breeding purposes and there is difficulty in safeguarding these large numbers in residential areas.

Anglers, therefore, have to rely on a limited number of commercial breeders, most of whom appear to be in business in North West England; where squatts were first used. The demand for squatts very much exceeds supply and they are virtually impossible to obtain in many areas of the country.

Years ago, when there was more horse-drawn transport, anglers could obtain squatts from stable manure and it was in this manure that they were first discovered. Because of its excessive heat, horse manure proved an ideal agent for breeding and in my early days of match fishing I used to collect squatts from manure heaps. This cannot be done today, apart from such places as racing stables where a number of horses are quartered together.

Due to the need for heat it is difficult for breeders to continue squatt production through the winter months. Some continue to breed, but the need for artificial heat increases production costs. Even so, squatts are now so popular that anglers will pay heavily to obtain them.

Almost every week the national angling newspapers tell stories of big match wins on bream rivers, which, almost without exception, are won by the use of squatts. It seems that anglers who fish without squatts on bream rivers and narrow canals have little chance of winning. It is this knowledge that has built up the demand, and breeders are turning over an increased amount of productive capacity to squatts. I don't breed them myself since I am totally committed to other maggots, but there are a number of large-scale breeders in Lancashire.

Squatts, being extremely light, cannot be loose-fed, except for the few occasions when fish are caught close to the rod end. They can be catapulted across a canal but, with this method of feeding barred in many areas, squatts have to be introduced to the water with the aid of cereal groundbait.

Being frail, squatts can be used in the groundbait in large numbers. I can put half a gallon of solid squatts into as little as seven pounds of groundbait. Thus, with the feeders so concentrated, there is not so much need to feed a swim heavily and with really large balls of cereal. This factor helps to keep the fish feeding.

Squatts, like gozzers and specials, soon turn into chrysalids, there-
re they must be kept as cool as possible and stored in fine damp
nd. Lancashire breeders have found the red foundry sand ideal but,
rictly, any fine sand will do. But it must be damp. Squatts can be
idged, but since they are so frail they must not be frozen and must
placed in an area of the fridge where the temperature is highest.

If I want to keep some in the fridge I take them out of the sand and
ut them into fine dry groundbait. Only fresh squatts can be stored
this way. Once they are getting towards the turning stage, they
ust be kept damp or they will float instead of sink. It is widely
ssumed that if squatts are kept overnight in damp groundbait they
ill float the following day. This is a fallacy, but at the same time it
n happen if the groundbait is too wet.

In fact there is the possibility of this happening to all maggots. If
ey are allowed to become very wet they seem to absorb not only
uantities of water but also an amount of air. When they do this
ey will not sink. To avoid this possibility, maggots should only be
dded to the groundbait at the water's edge when fishing is about to
gin.

I always riddle my squatts out of the sand at home before setting
ff to a match and replace the sand with a small quantity of damp
ran or fine groundbait. A tablespoonful to a pint of squatts is about
ght. I then store the squatts in a cloth bag equipped with a draw-
ring neck. This keeps them in good order and they are easily
acked in the fishing basket.

Under no circumstances should both the squatts and sand be put
to the groundbait. The squatts are placed into this foundry sand
y the breeder and, since they clean themselves in it, this holds a
rge proportion of filth that can only act as a deterent to fish.
nother point here is that the sand makes the groundbait too heavy—
hich should be avoided, since the heavier it is the greater the
rface impact and the greater scaring-effect it has on the fish.

The ideal riddle to remove the sand from the squatts is the same
eat-safe gauze used for the specials. The fine loose-grained sand
uickly drops through it, leaving the squatts and the tiny hard balls
f sand behind. I then leave the squatts and remaining rubbish on
p of the riddle overnight. In the morning the fresh and lively
uatts will have crawled through the mesh. Only the lumps of sand
d dead or poor-quality squatts are left behind. The result is that
e very best of the squatts have worked through and they are 100
r cent pure. I then put them into the cloth bags.

I am convinced that part of the value of the squatt as a feeder
aggot lies in the fact that its colour is very similar to the anatto

maggot which I often use with it. This colour-blend could be part c
the reason for the marked success of these two when used togethe:

There are a great many times when it is worthwhile using squatt
on the hook. When a bream shoal becomes shy, after yielding a fev
fish, a change to a hook baited with two or three squatts can ofte
produce a run of bites and more fish. Squatts are also a very usefu
bait and feed in canal fishing where the fish are small.

A little fish can eat many more squatts than pinkies and its intere:
can be maintained longer before it has had enough and ceases t
feed. The longer a fish can be made to have an active interest in th
feed the better its chances of being caught.

7. Other Hookbaits

Worms

WORMS ARE NOT a very popular bait among match anglers. They have, in fact, often been regarded as a bait only to be used when all else has failed. But during the last war, when foodstuffs could not be used as bait, and when no-one had the necessary spare time to devote to breeding good-quality hook and feeder maggots, we did achieve more than a measure of success using worms in the Plank Lane warm water stretch of the Leigh Canal. In winter sweepstakes match anglers found that the tail-end of a small redworm would often take good-quality roach. These tail-end baits were never very big. Most anglers used segments about double the length of the ordinary hook maggot.

From time to time a match or two was even won by anglers baiting in this way, the top catches running as high as 4 lb. When I saw this, I wondered if worm fishing could be transformed into a regular winning method by obtaining enough worms so that some could be used as feed.

I used to spend a little time each Monday collecting up to 200 redworms from manure heaps. I then cut them up into sections an inch long and put them into moss for the coming weekend.

By the weekend the cuts had healed and it was possible to nick the worms on to an 18 fine wire hook in the same way as with a maggot. They moved attractively when placed on the hook. I used to fish across the far side of the canal, slowly swimming the stream with an inverted porcupine quill which had a balsa tip set over the fine end of the quill. This was really the forerunner of the stick float, and I fished it 'double rubber'.

Using these segments of worm on the hook and feeding more worms in with my 'black magic' leaf mould, I won nineteen two-hour sweepstakes in succession. Weights were never high. My best weight was little more than 4 lb. but this technique produced roach on the 2 to 3 oz. mark, perch up to 4 oz., and small rudd and gudgeon. There were three occasions when I hooked biggish carp that would have won me the match on their own, but I was using only a 1½ lb. to 2 lb. breaking strain line and the carp nearly always broke free. I did manage to land one carp. It was a fish of 1 lb. 11 oz. and during

77

those nineteen matches I remember catching that same fish three times. I am sure it was the same fish, because it was exactly the same weight each time.

But, although I won these nineteen matches, I had to practise first before the winning run began and I used to spend many hours perfecting the technique. But this was only a winter method. During the summer months I reverted to maggot fishing, when it was possible to breed good-quality bait again. Nevertheless I am sure canal anglers could do just as well these days if they tried this method in winter.

The worm is one of the most natural of all our baits and makes a very good winter bait, particularly after heavy rain when the water is coloured. I must admit that I still prefer maggots, but I know matches have been won with worms in the Witham and if this has worked once there must be times when it will pay off again.

For the contest angler who goes over to Ireland to fish matches, the worm is a must. In those rivers large numbers of cut-up worms are vital for feed and can be introduced in groundbait. My son Kevin and I both fed with large numbers of worms during the Angling Times Winter Leagues final on the River Suck at Ballinasloe. We were drawn eighteen pegs apart and I caught a few bream at the start before their interest ceased. But Kevin was more fortunate and kept bream feeding throughout the match to end with a winning weight of 56 lb. 9 oz.

I am sure the same tactics would pay off when fishing for chub in the River Ribble, and the Severn too. I did try this out once during an afternoon's practice fishing on the Ribble. Using three-inch lengths of lobworm I had thirteen chub between 2 lb. and 3 lb. each, but I have never yet tried this in a match in a fast-flowing English river.

Match anglers should remember that although worms do sometimes produce a bite or two when it may have seemed the fish were not feeding, they can be a time-wasting bait. Sometimes a biggish bream will take a worm with relish when it has refused maggot, but this is not a bait to be used at random on each and every water. If practice fishing shows the fish will take worm then it is useful as a change bait, but nevertheless it must be considered very secondary when compared with the maggot.

Wasp Grubs

Wasp grub fishing, like caster fishing, has been a developing art in recent years. As every Severn matchman knows, some huge

atches of chub have been made on this bait, but the most improved
aspect has been the discovery of successful methods of swim feeding.

Wasp nests cannot be bought. Each angler has to find his own and
his takes a lot of time, and once the nests have been found they
cannot be dug out right away. It is necessary to wait until dusk when
all the wasps are back in the nest before applying the Cymag poison
which kills them. The nest is then left overnight and dug out next
day.

The wasp grub season is a very short one. It lasts only six weeks—
from August to mid-September. There are wasps flying around later
than the middle of September but by that time most of the grubs
have already hatched out into wasps and there are fewer grubs
remaining in each nest.

I think three nests are the absolute minimum. To go to a match
with the firm intention of fishing for chub with less is unlikely to
prove very successful.

The first task, once the nest has been dug out of the ground, is to
remove the big queen wasp grubs. These are the grubs to use as hookbait. But there are only between twenty and forty of these in each
nest, the number depending on the size of the nest. From three nests
there should be about 100 queen wasp grubs. These big grubs are
placed in dry bran and together with the remainder of the nest—
including the wood pulp nest casing—are popped into the fridge to
await the weekend's match.

On the night before the contest the nest is pulled to pieces with
the hands and then mixed into between fourteen and twenty pounds
of groundbait. The amount of groundbait used depends on the proportion of nest and grubs required. It is important to mix in the nest
itself as well as the grubs, for this seems to have a great power of
attraction to chub. The nest is sweet to the taste and I am sure this is
the key to its success.

I am, in fact, experimenting to see if it isn't possible to find sub-
stances that provide an identical flavour to wasp nests. If one can
be found it will take fish right through the season, for chub will feed
on this at any time and not just during the short period when there
are a lot of wasps about.

The balls of groundbait should be very solid and heavy. They have
to sink to the bottom in fast-flowing water and, since the nests have
been difficult to obtain, they cannot be wasted by allowing them to
be carried away downstream to someone else's swim.

The grubs for the hookbait can be used singly or with up to four
on the hook at a time. I think two is enough at any one time and use
them on a size 8 hook; a round bend with an offset point.

It would be wrong to assume that chub are the only fish that will feed on wasp grubs. I have caught bream on them. But wasp grubs are very large in relation to maggots and therefore it seems that fish with big mouths are more likely to take them.

But even though wasp grubs are a very killing bait, it is wrong to become too single-minded about them. In September 1967 my son Kevin and I managed to find and dig out no fewer than sixteen wasp nests for use in a single match. We took half each and went to the big Kidderminster-organised Wednesday businessmen's match, fished by about 200 anglers.

I was drawn just downstream of Bewdley bridge and it looked a fine chub swim to me. I caught a 6 oz. chub soon after the start and was hopeful of a run of bigger ones. I was prepared to wait but I kept getting tiny bites and couldn't hook a fish. With half the match gone I caught a dace and this prompted me to fish for them, changing over to baiting with casters. I began to catch dace in large numbers right away and ended the contest with 15 lb. 11 oz.

Had I fished the whole match with casters for dace—they ran between 2 oz. and 6 oz.—I would probably have won. This illustrates the point that wasp grubs can be too much of a fad. I wasted time fishing with grubs that day simply because I had taken a lot of trouble to get them and wanted to make use of them, if possible. Instead they were a confounded nuisance. I would have been better off never to have taken them but, of course, I might have drawn a swim containing lots of chub where they would have been invaluable.

Knowing which bait to use on each occasion is one of the secrets of success. It isn't always easy to make the right decision and on this occasion I was wrong.

It must be remembered that in rivers like the Severn the chub are not spread evenly through long lengths of the river. The fish shoal-up in favoured areas, rather like bream. Therefore the angler must know where he can expect to find chub. There is no point in fishing with wasp grubs in areas where chub are few or even non-existent.

It is beyond question that wasp grubs are an extremely fine bait for chub. If these were available throughout the season, catches would be very much higher than they are. Yet chub cannot naturally obtain wasp grubs to eat. These cannot possibly be carried into rivers. I believe there is some ingredient in the grub which appeals to chub. If this can eventually be identified and added to groundbait, big catches of chub will be made at all times of the year.

Cheese

Cheese is without doubt a good bait for some big fish, particularly chub and roach, but nothing will ever convince me that it is worth using in a match. It is a restrictive bait in that it will take only some species of fish. I want to be in with a chance of catching as many as possible each time I fish. Cheese is without question a very good bait for men who have free choice of swim along a large length of river bank. They can pick out the few spots where the bank is undercut or where there are willow trees providing attractive root cover for fish. They can offer cheese-baited hooks for a time in each spot, gradually moving along the bank getting a fish here and a fish there. This gives them some good sport but has nothing whatsoever to do with match fishing.

The match angler is obliged to fish in one position. He cannot move from place to place. He has to make the best of the stretch of water in front of him and this may be totally unsuitable for fishing with cheese. And even though there is just the chance it may be, I cannot restrict myself to fishing for a small number of bigger fish which I may or may not be able to tempt. I want to catch the dace as well as the chub, and to land whatever there is in front of me. So I have to use a bait which will appeal to the great majority rather than to a minority of the fish population. If I want to specialise for chub I use wasp grubs, when I can get them, but otherwise prefer casters on the hook. Cheese is not for me.

Bread

Bread is another bait that I find of little use in match angling. There are very few occasions when I cannot do better with some other bait.

Bread punch fishing has won a lot of matches in the canals in the North West but it is a restrictive bait and anglers rarely get top-class weights of fish using this method. It is a winner in small canal matches when the top weight is no more than 4 lb. but rarely comes off in the bigger open contests where heavier catches are required.

I have never regarded myself as a 'place' man. I fish all individual matches to win and that means rejecting the methods that limit my chances. Bread punch fishing is a speed method, but its drawback is that it is aimed at catching tiny fish. Most of the roach caught are fish in the $\frac{1}{2}$ oz. to 1 oz. range. Bigger fish are quite rare, even though oz. roach are taken from time to time. If form runs true. I would wager that the top three places in big open events will most often

F

go to men baiting with casters—and fourth place is not good enough
for me!

Bread punch fishing is a very delicate method of catching fish.
Hooks are usually either size 20 or 22, with only the tiniest fragment of
bait being punched out of a slice of bread with a punch made
especially for the job. Line sizes are of as little as 8 oz. breaking
strain. This means that in the unlikely event of a biggish fish being
hooked the line either breaks or the tiny hook pulls free.

I cannot condemn the method when it is used in small matches
where the winning target is only around a couple of pounds of fish,
but this sort of fishing doesn't appeal to me. I get no personal
pleasure from it.

On the bigger fisheries, the bream and chub rivers, bread does
catch fish from time to time, but it must be used with great caution
or large chunks of fishing time will be wasted. I would never go to a
contest and fish with bread on the hook as a wild gamble that the
fish will take it. I only consider baiting with bread if I have tried it
out on the same river the previous day and found it worthwhile.

There are times when bream will take bread in preference to maggot
at the start of a fishing season. At this time the bream haven't been
subjected to constant feeding with maggots and haven't become quite
so singleminded as they are from the middle of July onwards. Thus
bread may be worth using in the opening month of the season.

But I still prefer to fish with maggot. I am convinced that I can
do considerably better with bream on maggot than with any other
bait. Even so I have spent periods of practice fishing checking to see
just what can be done with bread. I have used it extensively on
Rudyard Lake and I can recall one catch of 40 lb. of bream that ran
to 2 lb. each. These are good bream for Rudyard, for most of the
bream caught there in contests are in the 12 oz. to 1½ lb. weigh
range. But there is a world of difference between pleasure fishing and
match fishing. When the man at the next peg is feeding heavily with
maggots there are few occasions when bread fishing is successful.

I remember one of my Leigh fishing colleagues telling me of a
30 lb. bream catch he had made on the Great Ouse Relief Channel
just prior to the 1967 National Championship. He had been pestered
by eels and they were continually snapping up his maggots. Nothing
can be more infuriating than a spell catching eels—which don't
count in most contests. This man changed over to bread and took
bream right away.

But one swallow doesn't make a summer and while match anglers
can succeed with bread from time to time I am sure it is often best
ignored altogether.

Bloodworms

Bloodworm is largely banned in British match fishing. It isn't allowed in the National Championship and only in a few areas of Lancashire, notably in the Wigan area, are bloodworm anglers allowed free rein. The ban came into existence largely because it was thought that bloodworms were only available to a small minority of anglers. It was felt, I am sure wrongly, that other anglers had no chance against this bait. Bloodworms are not banned on grounds that they are an unfair bait in themselves, and since fish can eat them naturally—as part of their daily diet—I can see nothing unfair about using them.

Bloodworms are no simple recipe for success. A man who uses them in a National Championship on a bream river would be handicapping himself, and certainly not gaining any advantage, for the bait is only useful in certain aspects of fishing.

All anglers can get themselves a supply of bloodworms if they are only prepared to take the trouble. I cannot see any valid reason why a man who is prepared to devote an afternoon to finding bloodworms should not be allowed to use them. It is up to him to decide where they are a practical bait and where they are not.

The only advantage in using bloodworms is that this bait allows anglers to catch large numbers of fish in quick time. But although the bait is extremely attractive to the fish in canals, little fish usually get to the bait first. The bigger fish—slower off the mark—are left standing by the little chaps. Bigger fish will take the bait, given the opportunity, and perch are particularly happy to feed on bloodworms. This bait rarely accounts for good-quality roach simply because they are beaten to the bait by smaller fish.

There has always been a strong fancy for bloodworm fishing in the Wigan area, the most popular waters being the Lancaster and Haigh canals. The method has been handed down from father to son in this area but its popularity has never succeeded in spreading about the country. There has never been any serious attempt to have the bloodworm ban lifted, mainly because the number of anglers involved is so small.

The bait was so effective in early days that the men who used it didn't really have to become exceptionally proficient canal anglers. The bait was so good for small fish that anglers could catch fish on despite technical limitations in presentation.

I took the trouble to check on the efficiency of the bait and decided it wasn't a serious threat when opposed to either caster or maggot fishing. As proof of this, I won a large number of matches in

which bloodworm anglers took part. The most notable of these wer
the Foster Memorial match on the Haigh Canal, with 500 men com
peting, and the Wigan Centre annual match, with a similar numbe
of contestants. All four top places were taken by men fishing wit
conventional baits. In the Haigh Canal event my team of fou
anglers weighed in over 16 lb. of fish—an all-time record for th
match and water.

This was proof enough for me that bloodworm fishing was n
serious threat to the methods I was using at the time. But the younge
generation of bloodworm anglers seem to have settled on bette
methods of presentation and are getting better results from it tha
their fathers used to do.

Instead of staying rigidly to a single bloodworm fished on a siz
20 hook, they have found that by switching to an 18 and using tw
bloodworms they can catch perch up to 12 oz. This has considerabl
increased the top limit of weights that can be attained by th
method.

Most matchmen will be aware of the huge number of fish th
French, Belgian and Italian anglers have been able to catch in th
annual Confederation Internationale de la Peche Sportive (Worl
Championship) matches. On occasions, these men have proved it
possible to take over 600 fish in three hours' fishing. I cannot se
myself either enjoying or even taking part in this sort of fishing, bu
we have to recognise that it is a method that may well catch on i
British match angling.

If, for example, we had put a team of bloodworm anglers into th
last World Championship to be fished in England—on the Rive
Thurne in 1966—England would have come very much closer t
winning than they did. As it was, our team suffered the indignity c
finishing no higher than eighth in a match they could have won.

The technique of fishing with bloodworms is simply a matter c
speed fishing. It is conducted close to the near bank and the angle
use short rods of no longer than ten feet together with centre-pi
reels—although the method is to fish so close to the bank that th
reel is rarely used.

The hook is a fine wire size 20 and the float either a tiny length c
peacock quill or a small crow quill, both of which are fished fro
the base only. They take no more than a single No. 4 shot. Feedir
is the all-important factor and this is carried out on the little an
very often principle. Usually the fish are taken with a falling bai
but if a bite has not been obtained during this period the angle
will leave the bait in a static position, expecting bites to follo
quickly.

For a three-hour canal match 400 bloodworms are sufficient for the hook; there are times when less will be ample. But nevertheless larger numbers are required so that some can be introduced as feed. The ideal amount is approximately a quarter of a pint. The biggest of the bloodworms are selected for the hook and kept fresh and lively in damp moss. A dessertspoonful of fine silver sand is added to the worms to be used as feed. This is to clean them. The bloodworms are placed into a mixture of fine leaf mould and groundbait on the bankside and watered down until the mixture is very sloppy.

This mixture is then thrown into the water close to the edge in small quantities and quickly brings the small fish around.

The keenest of the bloodworm anglers seek out supplies of immature bloodworms which they call 'jokers'. They prefer to use these as feed, rather than the bigger bloodworms which are then reserved for the hook.

Bloodworms are the larvae of the small mosquito or gnat. They are found in stagnant ponds and in the muddy, silted fringes of still-water lakes and in backwaters where there is no flow. They cannot be found on clean sandy-bedded waters since they prefer dirty water.

There is no problem in obtaining large numbers of bloodworms once they have been located. My method was to use a sharp-edged two-inch wide metal blade fitted on to a four-foot long broomstick. The metal blade was eighteen inches long and fastened at the extreme end of the stick, giving an overall length of five feet six inches. See Fig. 27. I used to take this device and cut into the muddy section of the pond with a sweeping action, so that the tip of the blade just touched the harder bottom of the pond during the sweep. As the blade was brought through the mud the edge contacted the blood-worms. The worms doubled over the blade and when it was brought out there were as many as twenty bent over the blade. These were simply wiped off the blade between finger and thumb and placed into a container. This simple method was continued until sufficient bloodworms had been obtained.

If no bloodworms have been brought out after a dozen sweeps with the blade it can be assumed there are either none there or not sufficient to make it worthwhile continuing. A new pond must be found.

There are one or two men who obtain supplies of bloodworms for Wigan and district tackle dealers by using fine-meshed nets similar to muslin. These fellows obtain the bloodworms for the hook as well as the immature worms that are used in that area as feed. These small worms are the best form of feed. However, the average angler who wants to sample bloodworm fishing just to see how effective it can be can quite conveniently do so by feeding his swim with bigger bloodworms.

A mature bloodworm is between three-quarters of an inch and one inch in length. It is a very tender worm and great care must be taken when putting one on a hook. The hooks must be very fine and extremely sharp, for otherwise the worm will burst and the liquid contents are lost. It is even a simple matter to burst a worm by pressure from the fingers. The hook is placed into the tail of the bloodworm where there is thicker and stronger segment. The hook is passed through the tail until the bloodworm lays in the middle of the round bend. Being so tender, the bait has to be changed after every bite; but otherwise can be used until it has been damaged by a fish.

FIG. 27
The tool used for obtaining bloodworms

8. Groundbait

N MY EARLIER DAYS of match fishing, when my fishing was largely onfined to Lancashire, I soon learned that groundbait had to be sed sparingly. With only the rarest of exceptions, it is impossible to atch big weights of fish in this area and anything over 10 lb. of fish 1 a match is very rare indeed.

The size of the fish is not so high as it is elsewhere in the country. ince Lancashire is largely an industrial area, pollution is more revalent and this tends to limit the growth of the fish. The fish are hy and difficult to catch, therefore groundbaiting has to be on a ery modest scale or the fish are soon over-fed and lose interest in he hookbait.

While I use small amounts of groundbait when canal fishing in rder to introduce squatts to the far bank area, this amount has to e kept to the minimum if the fish are to feed for the duration of a natch. That's one of the reasons why I prefer to introduce my loose eed by means of either a catapult or a throwing stick. But I cannot se these aids to feeding in all canals and there are times when I have o alternative to using a groundbait as a delivery agent for both quatts and casters.

I am very conscious when groundbaiting that my feed must not nake any undue surface commotion on impact. I therefore have to se a very light, fine groundbait which breaks on hitting the surface, hus reducing the violence of the impact. Frequently these canal wims are as little as one foot deep so this can be seen to be a crucial oint.

If I have to use groundbait in a three-hour canal match I never use nore than two pounds—often much less. The cereal itself is bread vhich has been put through a very fine riddle to ensure it is as fine as ossible. It is not good enough to mix the groundbait at the water-ide. It must be mixed ready-for-use at home before leaving for the ontest. The object in doing it so long before the start of the match is o be certain that the cereal has absorbed the water completely and hat it has had time to become soft and silky.

The balls that are thrown in are very small. Walnut-sized balls are est and the bait must have sufficient knitting-power to hold a dozen

squatts without breaking up when thrown. The average distance thi
has to be thrown is around forty feet and the ball must arrive on th
surface intact or the bait will be dispersed. Thus a fine balance ha
to be struck between the strength and ability of each ball to brea
up. I find that custard powder, added in very small quantities, help
the groundbait to hold together but doesn't clog it to the extent tha
the groundbait then sinks through the water with the ball still intact

As far as I have been able to discover there is nothing that can b
introduced to groundbait by way of an additive which in itself attract
the fish. The only positive attracting element, additional to th
groundbait itself, is the maggots or casters placed in it. But ther
are grounds for thinking that sweetened feed might prove attractiv
to some species—if not all of them.

Some clever match anglers put oil of aniseed in their groundbai
and others use sugar to add attractiveness. Whether this really work
I doubt if they can say with any certainty, but I do think that sweet
ness is useful. If this can tempt the fish into staying in the ground
baited area longer than would otherwise be the case there is a greate
probability of catching them. But it is almost impossible to be dog
matic and to say that this actually happens.

I am toying with the idea of mixing black treacle and brown suga
into groundbait intended for chub, in the hope that this will resembl
the taste and have the attractiveness of the wasp grub and its cake
This may never work but it is always worth trying these experiment
in the hope that something positive will emerge.

I very rarely use groundbait when fishing flowing rivers for roach
In waters like the Severn and Ribble, when after roach, I much prefe
to loose feed with casters, but there are times, particularly when th
water is coloured and the flow is strong, when groundbait is neces
sary. Only groundbait can get the feed down to the bottom quickl
enough to beat the extra pull of the flow. Under these condition
roach do not dart about in the water feeding at random. They ar
much slower and feed more steadily. Thus the hookbait has to b
moved more slowly through the water and the feed must do the same

Groundbait must always be mixed with the greatest care so that i
is neither sloppy nor dry; so that it neither disintegrates in the ai
nor floats on the water. I prefer to mix mine twice. First I overwe
it so that it is quite sloppy. I leave this for five minutes after the wate
has been added to give the feed a chance to fully absorb the moisture

Then I add more dry groundbait and keep mixing it in until I hav
reached the stage when the correct degree of dampness has bee
obtained. Incidentally, I never mix groundbait anywhere other tha
at the waterside except when canal fishing.

My groundbait must 'mush' when it hits the water. I want it to break up right away. But I know many anglers have difficulty in mixing a groundbait stiff enough to be thrown thirty yards and yet soft enough to break-up on impact with the surface.

There are one or two little 'wrinkles' that help. First of all, when I aim to feed a swim that is a very long way out I always put a proportion of bran in my groundbait. This can be as high as thirty per cent on a water like the Great Ouse Relief Channel. The bran prevents the ball from clogging and from becoming rock-hard.

Most important of all, always prepare a ball of groundbait for throwing with *wet* hands. The moisture on the hands allows the ball to be smoothed and for the outer casing to clog and bind. When the ball is actually thrown the hands must still be wet. Then the bait leaves the hand cleanly and flies accurately as required. If the hands are dry there is the tendency for the groundbait to stick to the hand. It can then neither be thrown so far nor so accurately.

As an alternative to groundbait as the delivery agent, I sometimes use what has become known as 'black magic'. There is nothing magical about it—after all, it is only common or garden leaf mould! The leaf mould should be light and silky. I put mine through a riddle to remove all the coarse pieces and then dry it off and store it until it is needed.

When I use it, I usually mix it with equal quantities of groundbait. This will then cloud the water, but not make those deathly white mushrooms that must scare the living daylights out of fish when they are the least bit sensitive. After all, fish may be used to taking food from coloured water but there is nothing natural about clouds of white groundbait.

All groundbait must be made to appear as natural as possible. The 'black magic' takes the whiteness off the feed.

I have never believed in paying fancy prices for groundbait. The cereal I use is the waste from a local bakery. It is the waste created when loaves are sliced. It doesn't get dirty and most bakeries are conscious of the fact that it makes good groundbait. They collect it and sell it quite cheaply.

But this is not all fine groundbait ready for immediate use and it pays to put it through a riddle to remove the larger sections of crust. This groundbait is not completely white, since inevitably it must contain a certain amount of fine crust, but nevertheless is still perfectly satisfactory for bream fishing. The colour of this bakery waste seems to vary from place to place. Some supply very white groundbait and in others it is much browner, but in any case I don't want absolutely pure-white groundbait. I believe fish are much more likely to accept an off-white or even brown feed—particularly in waters which are very clear.

In a five-hour match where bream are the target it is vital to have at least fourteen pounds of groundbait available in case of need. It isn't always necessary to use that much, but anglers must plan for the extreme days when a lot of feed is required. In the warm days of summer bream eat much more than they do in the cold of the winter. Thus anglers will need to feed more heavily in the warmer weather. This is a factor which should always be taken into account.

There are anglers even today who recklessly throw in the same amount of feed in every match they fish, without regard for the circumstances. I have fished the Witham, perhaps the heaviest-fed river in the country, for bream with as little as five pounds of groundbait in a day and kept the fish feeding. Had I used more I could very well have made them lose all interest.

There are many proprietary brands of groundbait on sale in tackle shops, selling in various grades of fineness. Most of these are top-quality feed and the only comment I make is that they seem rather expensive. But it is always better to buy in bulk. A hundredweight works out cheaper and the man who fishes every week is better served by having a stock at his home than in having to buy each week.

The dry groundbait can be stored in metal drums and will keep indefinitely. There is no need to fit a lid unless it is stored in a damp place or if it is subject to dust.

9. Legering

SENTIMENT AND SUCCESS have nothing in common. I much prefer boat fishing for personal pleasure and satisfaction, but match fishing to me means trying to win. There is no denying the fact that winning matches of bream are often taken on a leger. And the bigger the match the greater the chance it will be won with that style of fishing. In the last six years this has become an ever-increasing trend and no match angler worthy of the name can ignore it.

The successful methods of fishing for bream have always been by providing bream with a still bait. They are not the most active of fish. They will not chase a bait in the same way as roach often do. A bream likes time to make up its mind whether or not it approves of what it is about to eat and methods of fishing which do not allow the bream that time have never succeeded.

Bream fishing in matches as we know it today is a relatively new aspect. In the past match fishing was largely a matter of catching roach, but the value of fishing for and catching bream has become increasingly known. Bream are bigger than roach and, although they all too rarely give those sustained spells of keen feeding more often obtained from roach, they are a most sporting fish.

At first, bream fishing in contests differed very little from roach fishing. Anglers would merely set their float tackle that little bit deeper to hold the bait on the bottom and hope that bream would come along. But, with the fixed-spool reel replacing the centre pin, anglers found it a simple matter to cast further across rivers and still waters. They were able to reach and fish for the bream that could rarely be tempted to feed close in under the rod top.

With this longer casting it became necessary to evolve new techniques in order to present the bait still on the bottom of the river. It could always be done easily under the rod top but, with distances of as much as thirty yards involved, clearly new techniques were essential.

The first step was the use of small sliding lead bullets which were placed on the line and stopped by a dust spot. These bullets were big enough to hold the bait on the bottom, but anglers had to set their floats much deeper than the depth of the water in order to

91

prevent the float dragging the bait out of position. But there we
tactical difficulties. In the deeper rivers it was clearly impossible f
anglers to fish at long range simply because they could not set the
floats deep enough. A depth of sixteen feet cannot be effectively ca
with a thirteen foot rod and a fixed float.

So the next step forward was the sliding float. This simplified t
whole operation and proved extremely successful. Many big catch
of bream are made by it even now, eight years later. But sliding floa
did not solve all the problems, and on windy days, and on occasio
when there was greater flow, it proved impossible to do as well with
as under more favourable conditions.

Clearly something else was needed and the first steps were to di
pense with the float altogether and to leger-fish direct to the rod to
This proved reasonably effective on flowing rivers, but was not s
successful in still and slow-moving ones. Something more delica
was called for. Bream would rarely swim with the bait sufficiently t
move the rod top.

The next step forward was the swingtip designed by Jack Clayto
the Boston fishing-tackle dealer. Living in Fenland, Jack had firs
hand knowledge of the problem. He overcame it by fitting his ro
with what appeared to be a broken tip. A length of pliable plast
along which the line passed via two rod rings was fixed to the rod to
and Jack soon proved that with this pendulum-type indicator brea
felt less resistance and were caught in greater numbers.

The swingtip performed so well that there are now very few brea
anglers who do not possess one. This need was fully impressed upo
match anglers when the National Championship was won by me
using swingtips, both in 1966—by Roy Jarvis—and in 1967—t
Eddie Townsin.

Other developments saw the arrival of a butt-bite indicator, whe
the moving arm which provides the clue to a bite was brought fro
the tip to the butt joint. Further experiments resulted in the bu
indicator being moved out to the lower part of the middle joint
three-piece rods. Bites registered better when the indicator was i
that position.

But anglers are never satisfied and are always looking for furth
improvements. One result of this is a fine tip joint, thinned down to
much smaller diameter than hitherto. This tip requires less tensio
to move it and a feeding fish can reveal the fact that it is feedir
without having to apply so much tension as had been the case wit
the earlier rod-top legering.

Along with many others, I soon realised the advantages of the
new techniques. But, in my opinion, each one has some advantag

over the others and I would never choose one of these legering devices to the total exclusion of the remainder. I consider anglers who have opted for just one of these legering methods and use it all the time are not getting the best results.

The swingtip has not yet been superseded as the best device for legering for bream in deep, slow-moving water. While the flow on the Severn, for example, is far too fast for the swingtip—it was never claimed to be of use there—it proves first class on Fen drains. These drains were built solely with the object of getting rid of surplus water from the land. They remain operational and, at unpredictable times, the water is pumped off by drainage engineers. Thus what may have been a still water may suddenly be transformed into a moving one. When this happens anglers who may have been performing well with a butt-bite indicator suddenly find it ceases to be so effective.

But the swingtip remains a good bite indicator. The pull of the flow on the line moves the tip upwards until, in fast flow, it almost assumes the same angle as the line itself. But there still remains sufficient angle between line and tip for a biting fish to give an indication easily spotted by the angler. There is no need to put a lot of weight on to a swingtip in order to increase the angle between line and tip. In fact, if lead is added in the shape of lead wire, the fish then has to move this additional weight and bites are less pronounced. In heavy flow a lot of weight is required to keep the tip down—so much that this is not worthwhile. Better then to use the tip as the indicator but, when the flow is light but lifting the tip, some lead wire can be usefully added to give a stabilising effect.

The butt-bite indicator has to be weighted when used in a flowing river and in many cases it becomes impossible to add sufficient lead wire to the indicator arm to overcome the pull of the water.

The butt indicator is extremely sensitive at times when there is no flow at all. It has the additional advantage of being closer to the angler than is the swingtip and therefore bites are correspondingly easier to see and hit. The indicating arm of my own brand of indicator is made from peacock quill, and there is nothing more sensitive than that. In still water there's no doubt that the butt-bite indicator is the most effective.

The efficiency of the swingtip has been improved to some extent by protecting the tip from the wind by means of a plastic transparent shield. Some anglers have gone to the length of painting graduated markings on their wind shields with the intention of making it easier to spot the slightest movement. Personally, I cannot see how these graduated targets serve any useful purpose. Anglers should be concentrating sufficiently on what they are doing to be able to spot bites without these devices. The tip need only be set so that it is just touching the surface of the water and the slightest movement will register as a gap between water and tip. This, to my mind, is the best way of spotting bites. See Fig. 28.

If I am fishing a still water with a depth of eight feet or less then I go for the butt indicator every time. Conversely, if the water is twelve feet deep then it is the swingtip for me.

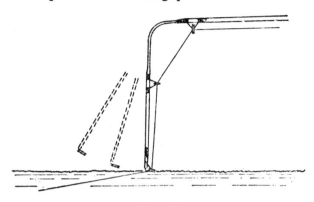

FIG. 28

A swingtip set to register bites. The tip rests against the surface of the water but a bite moves the tip away from the water. As soon as a gap shows between water and swingtip this indicates a fish has taken the bait

The great advantage of the butt-bite indicator is that it is fishing and detecting bites very much more quickly after the cast than the swingtip. On days when there are a lot of fish feeding and catches are high it is particularly valuable, since there is less fiddling about before the tackle is properly set and the bites begin to register. I also prefer the bite indicator when fishing with a four feet 'tail' between hook and bottom shot for fish that are taking the bait 'on the drop'.

These bites do not show in any really marked fashion on any leger method, but, at least, with the butt indicator, the registration is closer to hand. The indicator is more easily seen at the butt than at the tip of the rod. I believe one of the secrets of using a bite indicator is in keeping hold of the rod. Never drop it into a rod rest. If the line is kept taut all the time and the rod securely held, then the angler is in the position of being able to strike instantly.

Of course, nobody can hold a long rod for any length of time without feeling the strain and this is the reason why I think all egering rods should be relatively short. Eight feet is ample. This cuts own weight and makes fishing more comfortable. And most things hat do that also make fishing more effective.

The swingtip, as I have already said, works best in deep, slow-owing water. Under these conditions anglers can use a heavy bomb nd get the bait down quickly and save some of the time that would therwise be wasted. But in shallow water the surface impact of a eavy leger scares the fish away. Then I use the butt indicator and a maller bomb.

Legering is not a method that anglers can take to instantly. Just ke float fishing, it requires constant practice. Bream bites are lower than roach bites to develop and therefore easier to hit, but vith experience anglers can reach the stage when they can hook many f the roach that take their baits. Nobody would sit down at a match n a roach water and fish with a swingtip but, inevitably, when after ream, there will be a number of bites from roach in most waters.

These fish usually provide only a small proportion of the total atch—when the catch is good enough to figure in the prize list—but iey do represent an opportunity for an improved weight. There may e only four or five bites from roach in five hours, but these could roduce an extra pound of fish. Maybe that's only the equivalent of ne bream, but is still very much worth having. But roach bites can e very fast and anglers cannot afford to sit back and relax, waiting or those gentle nudges or slow pulls on the swingtip that come from ream.

Leger fishing direct to the rod top with a fine tip joint has come ito fashion on flowing rivers where the strength of flow is too great ither for the butt indicator or the swingtip. It is very useful on Fen aters when these are being drawn off and the water is moving, but is not so efficient as the other two methods of bite indication on till water.

It is really the third choice, but is still a very fine method on those aster-moving waters. The reduced tension in the fine tip, as opposed o the relative stiffness of the top joint fitted to most rods, means iat the tip sets into a bend with the pull of the water. But despite iking this bend, the tip remains sensitive enough to signal bites.

There are a number of different patterns of these tips. One takes ie form of the normal tip joint and is of the same length, but has a iuch sharper taper. Another is used as an extension to the existing od. It calls for a special male ferrule to be whipped on beside the ormal end ring. The ferrule can take a number of soft tips of varying trengths. The thinnest is used in slow-moving water and the thicker nes when the speed is greater.

Another method of legering, used under perfect conditions bu particularly effective when fish are only feeding shyly, is slack-lin legering. With this method the thickness of the rod top is unimportan After the leger has been cast out the line is tightened but then allowe to go slightly slack. There is no tension from the line on the tip an the line itself hangs in a slight arc.

Anglers watch the line for the bites and these are seen when th line straightens. The slack is taken up as the fish moves the lin Some men have developed this method to a very fine art and, o occasion, will watch the line at the point where it enters the wate When a bite comes the line is seen to twitch as it tightens. But I mu emphasise that this is for still days and dead water only. It cannot b applied at any other time.

There is no need to use heavy strengths of line for leger fishing. there are big fish about then this has to be taken into account, but can manage very well with a 2.6 lb. breaking strain line for most c my legering. It is worthwhile remembering that to use a thicker lir than is really necessary only adds to the weight and water resistanc that a fish has to overcome before registering its movements on th bite indicator.

The terminal tackle of the leger rig is most important. Unle this works properly there can be no registration on even the most del cately-set indicator. The rig has to be employed with the object c allowing each fish to take the bait and quickly signal that it ha done so.

The best leger weight itself needs little introduction. Most peop know what Arlesey bombs are. These bomb-shaped leads cast e tremely well, moving through the air with a minimum of resistanc Thus they can be cast more accurately than leger weights of ar other shape. They are ideal in still or slow-moving water and are the best possible shape to sink quickly once they have hit the surfac but they do tend to roll on the bottom in fast water. This may not b a bad thing when anglers want the bait to roll in an arc, taking th bait to fish which may be spread over an area of the bottom.

I do not often leger in really fast-moving water. I prefer to use float, but I do know that the coffin-lead has some advantages in suc places. It is a thin lead which can lay flat on the bottom and exposed to much less water resistance than the Arlesey bomb. Lil the Arlesey bomb, it can be bought in a variety of sizes.

I prefer simplicity above all else when deciding which is the be rig. I knot my leger weight on to a short length of the same breakir strain line as is used on the reel. This short length is then tied on t the reel line some eighteen inches from its end. When the knots hav een completed and the bomb and line are attached to the reel line his connecting link should be eight inches long. See Fig. 29.

The exact position where the connecting link is tied to the reel line aries. As I have already stated, I prefer my hooks to be tied to an ighteen inch length of nylon. Therefore, if I intend to fish with a istance of three feet between the hook and the link knot, I tie this not eighteen inches along the reel line. If I require to fish with a horter tail, then the distance is correspondingly reduced.

In the normal way, with bream taking the bait either just off or on he bottom, a distance of three feet between hook and knot is ideal. ut if the fish are feeding strongly off the bottom—and taking the ait before it hits bottom—there is a good case for increasing the gap etween knot and hook to as much as five feet. This means the bait inks through a greater depth of water once the weight has hit bottom he falling bait is often extremely attractive to bream, particularly n the summer when the fish are more active.

A word of warning though. Once the bait has dropped on to the ottom, the greater distance between hook and link means that a ream can pick up the bait and move around without giving any ndication of what is happening. It is not until the fish exerts tension n the indicator after tightening all the slack line that bites can egister. A fine balance must be struck to ensure that the 'tail' is kept o the ideal length so that all bites register.

Bearing in mind that fish can often strip a maggot when allowed long tail with the bait on the bottom, there is a strong case for hortening the length of tail if the maggots are found to be sucked et no bite seen. When the water temperature is low the fish do not wim so freely as when it is higher. Thus winter bream fishing usually alls for a shorter distance between hook and link than in summer. his distance can at times be reduced to as little as two feet but on his type of rig there is no point in shortening any further. But emember, this is only for fish feeding on the bottom.

As an alternative to knotting the paternoster link to the reel line ome anglers employ a small swivel. One end of the link ties to one ye of the swivel and the other eye runs along the reel line. It is ocked into position with a stop shot which determines the length of he tail. The one advantage in this method is that one needs to do no ore than move the stop shot to alter the length of the tail. This kes less time than cutting off and retying the knot. But, to my mind, his advantage is offset by the fact that the bream has to move the eight of the stop shot and the swivel. Thus the feeding fish feels more esistance and is less likely to continue to take the bait. See Fig. 30.

A further alternative, often used, is to dispense with the nylon

G

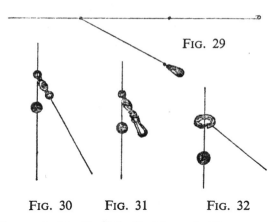

FIG. 29

FIG. 30   FIG. 31   FIG. 32

The terminal tackle of the ideal leger rig. There are only
two knots and no weight on the line. A fish can take the
bait and feel no resistance (*Fig. 29*). Alternative terminal tackles. All of these are inferior to Fig. 29 and in
each case the fish has to move a shot before registering
the bite (*Figs. 30, 31 and 32*)

link altogether and to clip the weight direct to a small link swiv
I think this is an even worse method. The fish's movements do n
register so well and with the bomb being so close to the reel li
greater resistance is imposed. There is also the disadvantage of t
fish having to move both the stop shot and link swivel. See Fig. 3

Attempts to overcome the disadvantage of the weight of tl
swivel have led to the use of fine alloy split rings. The link is knott
to the ring and the reel line runs through the eye of the ring. S
Fig. 32. As a further means of reducing weight a rubber stop has be
tried in place of the stop shot. This is quite effective but,
occasions, I have had false bites that led nowhere. I came to t
conclusion that the fish must have been mouthing the rubber stc

These false bites cannot be eliminated by using inconspicuous
coloured rubber. Red rubber is obviously more likely to be pick
up by a fish, but they will even pick up a short length of black rubb
They won't swallow it but will mouth it before rejecting it. If t
fishes' attention is allowed to be diverted from the hookbait in a
way this automatically reduces the chances of getting them into t
keepnet!

Legering is still in its infancy. New techniques are developing
the time, but it has not yet reached the stage where it is possible

in a match legering for roach and dace in rivers like the Trent. Match fishing can be simply assessed as a matter of getting a fish from every bite. Nothing less is good enough. And, at present, no legering method allows a matchman to hook small fish consistently in fast-moving rivers. Therefore float fishing is still more effective. I am sure the time will come when we have been able to devise a method of catching small fish quickly on a leger.

The Trent is a river prone to flooding, and when this happens, anglers are frequently forced back many yards from what is normally the water's edge. Consequently they fish from positions where there may be a wide expanse of very shallow water in front of them which incapable of holding fish. Faced with a situation like this anglers would do as well with the leger as with any other method. They could never hope to catch enough fish to win with a decent weight, but, when team fishing, they could catch just those few fish which make all the difference between success and failure. Trent fishing is usually confined to between one and three rod lengths out. Even with legering there won't often be need to cast further.

Anglers are often all too ready to accept that there are no fish in their swims. When fishing is difficult and the water seems barren many men will resign themselves to a very poor, if not a completely blank, day. Yet this need not be so. I was fishing one of the Trent Saturday Sweepstakes in 1966. The river was flooded and I couldn't get a bite. Instead of accepting what seemed a hopeless situation I decided to leger to see if I could get a fish or two. I set up leger tackle, fishing direct from the rod top.

In half an hour I had between fifteen and eighteen bites. I didn't hook one of them—which underlines the difficulties that still need solution. But there were fish in that swim. The problem was that I was using caster on the hook and this bait produces fast bites. The bites I had came so quickly that I had no chance of connecting with them, even though I was keyed to the task and holding the rod ready for an instant strike. But try as I did I couldn't hit them fast enough.

When leger fishing techniques have further improved it will be possible to take fish that feed in this way. On this occasion I might have had a fish or two had I switched to baiting with maggot, but I was determined to make every effort to succeed with casters. Despite the utmost concentration, I failed.

In most canals, where the stock is of small fish, there is no point legering. But in canals that hold bream and other good-sized fish is sometimes sensible to try a leger. I am thinking in particular of swims in the wide basins that were built as loading bays and mooring points for barges. In these places canals are as much as three times

their normal width. These are the places that usually contain a
bream there may be in the water. The other bigger fish also pre
these wide waters to the narrow sections. In a situation like this
sensitive butt-bite indicator could give good results.

I can recall situations years ago when, had I used an indicator
would have caught many more of these bigger fish than I did. But,
course, legering, as we know it today, didn't exist. In 1966 wh
fishing a match on the Warrington Canal I float-fished from t
start and had caught nearly 4 lb. of fish. But the weather deteriorat
and a strong wind started to blow into my face. This upset t
method I was using and, since I needed very little more to be sure
winning, I put on my butt indicator. After ten minutes this broug
me one fish—a perch of about 12 oz. I weighed in 4 lb. 11 oz. a
won the match with four ounces to spare. In other words, if I had n
switched to legering I would not have won.

Legering comes into its own on the bigger bream rivers, pri
examples being the Welland, the Witham, Relief Channel a
Middle Level. It is frequently said by anglers who catch, or shou
have caught, bream in matches fished on these and similar wat
that the bites were the tiniest of nudges on the indicator. I cann
accept that these are the best bites it is possible to obtain.

Except in winter, when bream do not move very far when feedi
I am sure that the fish's action in taking the bait into his mouth
always the same. Therefore I believe that the bites should always
positive and that, if this is not the case, there is something wro
with the tackle being used. It may be the terminal rig or the indicat
but, whatever it is, there is a fault somewhere. If this is found a
eradicated then the bites will show more positively.

The terminal tackle I have previously mentioned, used with
correct indicator, should ensure that the bites are positive, but
rod must always be positioned correctly or this advantage can
lost. With the butt indicator the rod must be positioned so that i
pointed straight towards the lead on the bottom of the water. T
more directly the rod is pointed at the weight the less a fish has
move the bait before causing the indicator to move. The rod is th
in a position where, when a bite develops, the angler can str
upwards and easily, without strain. There is no slack line and
fish should be hooked at once.

In the early stages of a match I begin by fishing with a single m
got on a size 18 hook. I find that these hooks are capable of deali
with any fish I am likely to encounter in a bream river. But I do ins
that, while I like to have as fine a hook as possible, it must be stro
enough not to spring outwards and open up, allowing the fish

get off. Since I shall be feeding with groundbait laced with squatts, it is most probable that I shall use an anatto hook maggot.

If bites start coming and the fish are of good size then I use two maggots on the same size 18 hook. If the fish are feeding strongly I change the hook to a 16. Never let a hooked fish take charge of the situation. Once it's hooked the angler must be boss. I don't mean that anglers should do anything rash. Big fish cannot be drawn into the landing net right away, but maximum pressure must be applied.

The object is not only to get the fish out quickly but also get it away from the spot where it has been hooked. If a hooked fish is allowed to dive and turn in the swim it will frighten the remainder of the shoal and there won't be much chance of catching any more.

The best way of landing a hooked bream quickly, once it has been drawn away from the groundbaited area, is to continue retrieving. The fish will then swim naturally and easily towards the bank. When the fish is close to the rod top it is then—and not before—brought to the surface. Once it shows on the surface, the rod is moved sideways to lay the fish over on its flanks. In that position it is incapable of further resistance and is drawn into the landing net.

The keepnet must be set in such a position that the fish can be popped into it with the angler having neither to actually get up from his basket nor to bend down. The head of the keepnet should always be close to the spot where the bream will be taken from the landing net. We all know of instances where good fish have been lost through a failure to do this. If the keepnet is in a handy position this also saves time.

There is a danger in that anglers are often tempted to lift out the small 3 oz. to 4 oz. bream with the rod and not use the landing net. These small fish have much softer mouths than the 1 lb. to 4 lb. bream. It pays to net every one, almost irrespective of size; only when they are of 2 oz. or less can they be lifted out on the rod with confidence.

There is not very much difference in my groundbaiting technique on any of these still or slow-moving bream rivers. I usually start with three tennis-ball sized pieces. This is sufficient to interest the fish that may already be in the swim and for the first quarter of an hour I fish over this groundbait. There is no point in bombarding with feed until the fish are either driven away or fed up with it. Once I start catching fish I give them as little feed as possible, but I throw in tennis-ball sized pieces with sufficient regularity to keep the fish concentrated in a small area.

I prefer to throw in my groundbait just before I cast, so that the leger bomb follows the groundbait down to the bed of the river. If the groundbait and the lead weight both arrive on the bottom at the same time this is just what's needed. This brings bites very much quicker than if the casting and feeding are done independently without regard for each other. This won't be successful for every cast of the match but it can produce a spell of anything between a few minutes and a couple of hours—on rare occasions even more—when fish after fish is hooked.

There is no point in throwing in more groundbait if fish are not feeding. I remain content with those first three balls and fish where this has fallen for about half an hour. During that time I try to catch fish by slowly moving the bait across the bottom. I wind the reel handle slightly, moving the bait about three inches at a time, until the hook has been drawn through the baited area. The same effect, of tempting fish into feeding, can be achieved by lifting and jerking the rod top. The bait can then be made to move up slightly from the bottom without disturbing the bomb.

If this hasn't brought fish after thirty minutes I throw in more groundbait, throwing in single balls and hoping to attract the fish by means of the cloud of feed that falls towards the bottom. This is repeated every ten minutes. Each time I let my bomb fall with the groundbait and then edge it through the swim.

I won't add any more feed than I have to. As long as I am catching fish with this slow-moving dodge I am happy with the situation. Only when it fails will I feed again. I continue this policy throughout the match, but if bites become more regular then I am obliged to give the fish more feed.

When the match begins I wet about three pounds of dry groundbait in my mixing bowl. Once I am satisfied that this is properly mixed I then add about a pint of solid squatts. In addition, I put in a couple of dozen hook maggots to give the fish a taste of the hookbait. It is of importance to continually mix the squatts and maggots with the groundbait. If the groundbait is taken from the top of the bowl each time it is needed the squatts will have crawled through the feed and will remain in the bottom of the bowl. Thus, in the first instance, the swim will be fed with groundbait containing few maggots and, later on, as the bowl empties, there will be so many of them that the groundbait cannot be thrown without breaking up in mid-air. Care should be taken to see that the ratio of maggots to groundbait remains the same throughout the match.

The size of the bowl in which the bait is mixed is very important. It is much easier to make up a perfect feed in a shallow bowl than in a deep one. The mix is then very much more even. The ideal bowl is of plastic. The best ones fit the inside diameter of the tackle basket and can be used as a tray to carry bait tins, thus not wasting valuable space.

It is not always easy to assess the amount of flow on these big bream rivers. The Ten Mile Bank length of the Great Ouse is very deep water. When it is flowing the groundbait can be carried as much as six yards downstream before it settles on to the bottom. In this sort of situation I prefer to use a small Arlesey bomb of as little as $\frac{1}{4}$ oz. I overcast the spot where the groundbait had hit the water and then let the bomb settle to the bottom on free line. The action of the flow moves the bomb downstream in an arc and it must therefore intersect the groundbait at one point. If the bomb rolls too much, passing through the groundbait and still moving inshore, then I change to a bigger bomb until I settle on the right size.

10. Float Fishing

THERE ARE MANY match anglers who are only competent at one typ
of fishing. They may be masters of that particular craft, but if the
have to fish in waters where their standard style cannot produce fis
then they are soon struggling. Float fishing can be divided, and eve
sub-divided, into a number of styles which are all effective o
occasions but which all fail on others. Therefore the successful matc
angler must not only be capable of telling almost at a glance wha
tactics to use, he must also be fully conversant with each method.

Range, depth, flow, fish stock, water colour—or lack of it–
temperature and season of the year: all these factors combine i
countless permutations to provide the problems that anglers mee
when they arrive at the waterside. I have spent a lifetime in anglin
looking for solutions to these problems and can claim to hav
succeeded in many cases. It isn't always possible to catch fish bu
the wider the experience, the greater the knowledge, and the bette
prepared a match angler will be.

In much canal fishing—and in this case the Lancaster Canal is
prime example—tactics have to be directed to catching small fisI
Whether we like it or not we have to fish with size 20 hooks for sma
roach and other tiny fish.

In the North West my standard technique is to use a tiny lengt
of peacock quill, one and a half inches long, as a float. Into this :
built the equivalent of one No. 4 shot for counterbalance, leavin
one No. 6 shot for the line itself. This tackle cannot be cast very fa
Its basic purpose is to fish the weeded fringes of the near bank. T
avoid disturbance and to get the bait to drop in the right wa
casting is underhand.

The small amount of groundbait required is mixed very wet an
in fact, is quite sloppy. It's rather like cake mixture before it
baked. This sort of feed makes instant cloud but this is useless i
itself. It must have an added attraction. This takes the form of nea
squatts, which are thrown in on top of the cloud. The hookbait is
single squatt, and when you remember that one squatt is about ha
the size of a pinkie you can't fish much finer than that!

But there are a small number of canals that hold a bigger stam of fish. I know the Oxford Canal is one of these but from my own experience I believe the Trent and Mersey Canal is one of the very best. It is ideal match fishing water and I particularly like the length between Weston and Stone. This is Stoke City A.A. water.

Since the fish are of a better size, it pays to use different tactics from those on the usual run of canals. To get the best out of the water it pays to fish near the far bank. I like to get my float six inches from the bank, fishing only nine inches deep. When I first fished this canal I tried out my normal canal tactics. With this method I found that I could just about top 5 lb. in a contest. This was often good enough to be a winning weight, but I thought the canal would respond to caster fishing. The very first time I gave it a try I had a very comfortable win with an excellent weight of 11 lb. 9 oz.

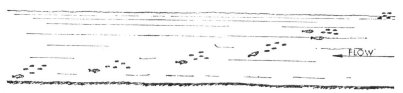

FIG. 33

How loose-feeding with maggots or casters gradually moves the fish upstream until they are feeding either in mid-water or near the surface and taking the bait on the drop

There are some fine bream shoals in this water. I don't believe they require any specific method that differs from the general pattern of my fishing in order to catch them. They, just like roach, can be induced to take casters fished on the drop; that is, when the bait is still sinking after the cast. See Fig. 33.

It is amazing what you can make fish do by sustained and accurate feeding. I once caught a 2½ oz. rudd here while my bait was actually out of the water. I had overcast and my bait landed, fortunately, on what was clear bank on the far shore. Before I could draw it back into the water the rudd popped out of the water, jumped three or four inches up the bank and took the bait!

On that occasion I had been fishing and feeding with casters. I had been putting them across the canal with a throwing stick and some had over-shot the mark and landed on the far shore. Fish had already taken some of the casters that were lying very close to the water and it was not surprising that, once they had become confident, one should jump up the bank to take my baited hook.

To fish the far side of a canal I use one of my cane and balsa stick floats. This takes two BB shot. I place these tight under the float and this still leaves enough buoyancy for a No. 8 shot down the line. One of the greatest problems in fishing these still-water canals and drains is surface drift. The water is still underneath but, by the action of the wind, the top of the water is moving.

I never let surface drift worry me. My style is not one where I want to hang on by the far shore for a long while until a bite comes. When fishing for bites from a sinking bait I can ignore the drift. By the time the line has been bowed the bait has sunk to the full extent and it is time to retrieve and cast again. I must emphasise, however, that for this style anglers must fish what I call 'double rubber'. This means that the line is fixed top and bottom to the float. To attempt this style with the line fastened only at the base of the float spells a succession of missed bites.

When anglers want to fish a 'hanging on' style and wait for their bites, then it pays to use a sensitive peacock quill float with a small cork body situated near the base of the stem. With this set-up I place two shot, usually two AAA, one each side of the float but, nevertheless, close together. This has the effect of setting the float immediately it drops on to the surface.

This cork-bodied quill float is mainly used in wide lengths where the water is shallow and where the two AAA shot are needed to supply casting weight. A quill without a body would be of an impractical length if it is required to take two AAA shot. Bearing in mind that the water is only from nine to eighteen inches deep, a float longer than four inches is a handicap. It would pierce the water on impact and scare the fish away. Therefore a cork body is essential in reducing the overall length to reasonable proportions for canal fishing.

As soon as the float hits the surface anglers must push their rod tips under the water and very quickly reel in about eighteen inches of line. This has the effect of sinking half the line. A portion over the centre of the water remains on the surface. I don't worry about this for the time being, but as soon as the drift starts to pull at the float then I give the line two or three sharp twitches—with the rod top low—and this takes down the remainder of the line. Usually this final sinking of the line comes about thirty seconds after the cast was first made.

One point I must emphasise is that when fishing casters by the far bank I never put my casters into groundbait. Remember, I want to catch the fish quite close to the surface. If I or anyone else use ground-bait, that takes the fish down towards the bottom and ruins the whole

ntention. Better to feed half a dozen loose casters regularly. I throw
my casters first, then quickly cast over them, bringing the float back
very slightly so that the caster on the hook is actually falling at the
same time and in the same place as the loose feed.

When fishing with a double rubber—the float fastened top and
bottom to the line—and with only light shotting down below—it is
vital to take advantage of the wind, using it to make certain that your
terminal tackle sinks its full depth without pulling the float out of
position.

If the wind is blowing along the canal from left to right I cast from
the right. If it is blowing in the opposite direction I cast from the left.
The object is to take advantage of the effect of the wind on the
terminal tackle so that this doesn't tangle with the float. It means that
I am casting into the wind at an angle and that the terminal tackle is
blown sideways and cannot touch the float in flight. When it hits the
water the terminal tackle lays across the surface parallel with the
bank. This allows the hook to sink close to the far bank, whereas if
the cast had been made down the wind the hook would have swung
away from the bank as it sank. See Fig. 34.

Of all the flowing rivers in the matchman's circuit, the Trent and
Calder are two of the most popular. But, while they call for tactics
differing greatly from those on rivers like the Severn, a man who
can catch fish regularly on those two can do so in many other rivers.
The Trent is a much shallower river than the Severn, though it has a
very substantial flow. The basic difference in fishing styles for the two
rivers is that anglers can use finer tackle to fish the Trent. In both the
Trent and Calder anglers can predict what they are likely to catch
with almost complete accuracy. On the Severn and Hampshire Avon
catches are much less predictable and there is always a need to take
into account the possibility of hooking really big fish.

The upper limit on the Trent and Calder is 12 oz. roach. There are
few other species to interfere with the reckoning. On the other two
rivers there are chub and barbel in good number spread pretty well
all along and these can never be completely discounted.

So, for a start, you know where you are with the Trent and Calder.
There is no need to use anything stronger than a 1½ lb. bottom. I
use that with a 2.6 lb. reel line. Fishing the Trent can be hard work.
Anglers must be 'on the go' all the time and for that reason tackle
must be comfortable to handle.

I prefer a twelve foot rod. The extra length of a bigger rod means
greater weight and finally discomfort. That to me spells missed
chances. Absolute efficiency is a must with all the tackle, for on both
the Trent and the Calder speed is important. Baits, like the fish you

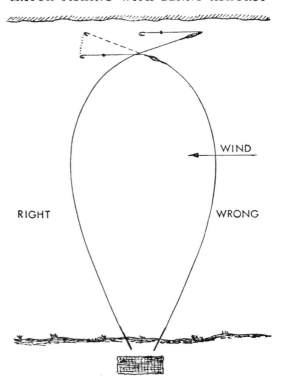

FIG. 34

The right and wrong ways of casting. Casting into the
wind means that the float precedes the bait and that the
baited hook sinks much closer to the far bank than
when casting is carried out down-wind. The extra distance gained by casting into the wind can mean a few
extra bites on days when fish are feeding very close to
the far bank

will be catching, are predetermined. There is no need to mess about
All you want are casters, anattoes and squatts.

The latter two are only a last resort. It is most unlikely that you
will ever win an individual event with them. They are merely a reserve
bait for use on days when casters prove unpopular. On the worst
days it may be possible to take a fish or two on maggots to boost a
team weight.

But casters are the bait to provide winning catches for individuals

They are the ones on which anglers must concentrate. The hook to use with them is a size 18 spade-end. I much prefer to use an all-black float. Mine take four No. 6 shot and are, of course, my balsa and cane favourites. I do not believe in bunching shot, I spread them evenly between the top of the eighteen inch bottom and the base of the float. See Fig. 7.

Bearing in mind that the Trent is usually some three feet six inches deep where you will be fishing, this means the shot will be eight inches apart. This even spacing means that you get good lift bite indications. When the shot are in position only the merest tip of the float is left above surface, but I always maintain a degree of lift on the float from the rod top and this brings a little more of the float above the surface.

I am sure that both Trent and Calder call for a cereal ground-baiting—particularly at the start of a contest. I drop in three or four golf-ball-sized pieces into which I have mixed a number of casters. But care must be taken when feeding casters in this way. If the balls of groundbait are nipped too much the casters will be crushed and destroyed.

The object must be to have the balls of groundbait break up at half-depth, ejecting the casters into the stream, but since they will then be through the fastest of the moving water they will sink quite quickly from thereon under their own weight. This sort of feeding at the start of a contest helps to concentrate the fish at the head of the swim. The object of all swim-feeding must be to gradually shorten the distance of the trot until the fish are swimming close to the bank —not far from the keepnet!

I start by fishing exactly the same depth as the river, but, bearing in mind that the rivers are flowing, the bait is always well off the bottom. The float is fastened top and bottom on the line. Nothing can convince me that a man who 'peg-legs it' (fastened at the base only) will not miss a far greater number of bites.

After the initial swim-feeding with cereals, it is time to begin loose feeding with casters. Take care not to throw these too far out into the stream or they will be swept downriver and out of the lower limit of your swim. The object must be to feed the very edge of the flow.

Do not be afraid to trot the full length of the swim. It takes much longer to catch fish at the end of the trot but you must find out where they are.

If you then find the fish are not being drawn upriver by your loose feeding do not throw the casters so far out. If you shorten the distance you throw them, they will automatically fall into slow-moving water and will sink more quickly. Thus the fish have to move upriver to take them. See Fig. 35.

As this tactic succeeds you will move the fish up to an under-the-rod position. This is the time to catch a lot of fish quickly. Look for your bites while the bait is still sinking. Keep the fish in this position by feeding with fewer casters at each throw, but do so more regularly. Never let the fish move away downstream again.

If the fish you are catching are small—and do not compare to those being caught by your neighbours—bring your float up the line a little. Sometimes the better fish lay a little deeper in the water.

If this fails, fish a yard or two further out into the stream. Do not loose feed that position, but put your casters in groundbait so that they sink quickly and keep your swim compact.

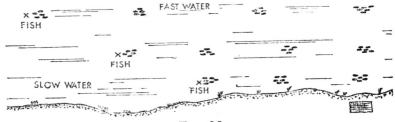

FIG. 35

When loose feed is thrown far out into a flowing river it is carried further downstream than when it is thrown in close to the near bank. If the fish are feeding a long way down the swim, maggots or casters thrown close to the bank can move them upriver to a position where they can be caught much more quickly

Match-fishing tactics on deep, fast-flowing rivers holding a good head of big fish are very different to those needed on the Trent. The tactics I now intend to describe are basically for the Severn in its middle and lower reaches, and the Hampshire Avon. They would, of course, also apply to some stretches of other rivers where circumstances are similar.

My ideal float is a porcupine quill—but with modifications. I choose the thickest porcupines I can obtain, using a quill eight to ten inches long. To the tip of the quill I fit a length of balsa. This is glued in position and then fined down and sandpapered until the wood merges with the shape of the quill. This sort of float, constructed on the same lines as my cane and balsa stick floats, has then the ideal amount of stability to ride the current. It has the

bility to set quickly after casting and also, a porcupine quill being
heavy, has the necessary casting weight. See Fig. 36.

The ideal shot-carrying capacity is three AAA shot. These should
be strung out down the line between float and hook and in no
circumstances should they ever be bunched together. If the shot are

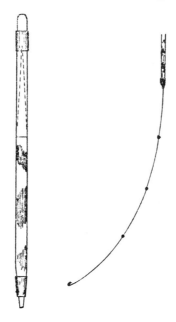

FIG. 36   FIG. 37

A porcupine quill inverted and tipped with balsa makes
an ideal float for fast-flowing rivers (*Fig. 36*). The even
distribution of the three AAA shot required to set the
float in Fig. 36. This method of shotting leads to better
bite indication in flowing rivers (*Fig. 37*)

bunched, lift bites will never register. If the shot are kept between nine
inches and one foot apart then lifts will show. The lower shot should
be eighteen inches from the hook. See Fig. 37.

For the Severn the hook must be a size 16, baited with two
maggots. The very first swim down could well result in a chub taking
and you must be equipped to cope. Allow the float to follow a
straight course, letting it ride downstream naturally with the flow.
You must make the bait on the hook appear every bit as attractive as

those loose maggots or casters that you will have been throwing in
If you fail the fish will be quite happy to take their fill of the free
offerings and will ignore the hookbait completely.

Swim-feeding is an art of its own. Start off with this loose feeding
with maggots or casters, the final choice depending on the swim you
are fishing and water conditions at the time. Having trotted through
the swim half a dozen times searching for that early chub, you now
have to try to concentrate your fish where it is convenient to hook
them out. And that's as close to your keepnet as you can make it!

At this stage you introduce something more substantial by way of
feed. Put in three good balls of fast-sinking groundbait that has been
liberally laced with maggots. This has the object of providing
attraction at the head of your swim in the spot where it suits you
best for the fish to take the hookbait. But after putting in the cereal
feed you must revert to loose feeding.

As you steadily build up the head of roach, dace, and perhaps
chub, at the head of your swim, you will find you will begin to take
fish on the drop—when the bait is still sinking through the water—
after you have cast. As soon as you can begin to see fish coming in
this fashion you are half-way towards winning.

Now is the time for a quick change of tackle. Three AAA shot are
really far too heavy to take fish consistently on the drop. Remove the
existing float and replace it with a stick (cane and balsa) float taking
three BB shot. But while this change is being made do not ignore
your swim. You have brought the fish close to the surface into this
on-the-drop position and you must keep them there. Any relaxing of
the loose feed and they will disperse again. So keep throwing in
casters or maggots as though you were still actually fishing.

When the tackle changes have been made you can carry on catching fish as though there had been no pause. Remember, the three BB
shot will have to have been spaced out evenly through the depth in
the same way as the three AAA had been.

Whereas you were throwing in a score or so of maggots or casters
at a time for loose feed, you must now speed up the rate of feeding
but reduce the amount. In other words, still put the same amount in
but instead of putting them in twenty at a time, throw in half a
dozen or so three times every cast.

If you have played your cards right you should get the fish on the
first drop, but that doesn't always work. If you don't get a bite
complete the first drop and then let your float trot a fraction before
holding it back. When you do this the rush of water forces your bait
back towards the surface. Once you have brought the bait back near
the top then let the float run a little and the bait will begin to sink

gain. Thus you can fish the on the drop technique twice or even three times with each cast.

But you should always keep a degree of tension from your rod top to the float. Once the fish are where you want them never let the float swim free. This holding up of the float accentuates the bites. Instead of toying with the bait the fish take decisively.

Always fish the deepest channel you can find in front of you. The fish are almost certain to be in it. Remember that in fast-moving rivers the shoals are nearly always on the move, hunting for food. Fish are canny creatures; they have to be to survive. When these rivers are in flood the fish frequently move out of the main river on to the flooded meadows. It is very rare indeed for anglers ever to find fish that have been trapped. The fish know exactly what is happening to the water level all the time, and they know this from the current. They cannot tell what is happening by staying in the dead, unmoving water.

Let this be your cue for action. It surely suggests that it is the faster-moving reaches that hold the fish and that dead water holds little or nothing. Of course, there are weather conditions under which fish are inclined to ignore the fast water. The bulk of these come with cold, frosty conditions and clear water.

On such occasions, when bites are likely to be scarce, it pays to leger. Bites register by the rod top straightening. I have proved this to be the case on most flowing rivers. On the Dee I once took fifteen dace in rapid succession when men using float tackle were not getting bites.

For this sort of fishing I much prefer the line to have a direct pull through the leger weight itself, rather than some form of paternoster fishing. With my method, I am sure the bait lies correctly in the water and the bites register much better. As an alternative to legering in frosty conditions it sometimes pays to float-fish, but with the float over-shotted by as much as an AAA shot. The bait is kept stationary, or as near it as possible, by holding the line tight to the rod top. When bites come to this method they will be very good ones. At all times, one point you must bear in mind is that the hookbait must be where the loose feed is. Only baits offered in this area will be taken with any regularity.

When you can do it, on the drop fishing for roach and dace is ideal. It will win many matches and is even capable of beating catches of chub. If I hook a 3 lb. chub naturally I want to get it out but, once the roach, dace and smaller chub are 'mad on', the sheer speed of it soon makes a winning weight.

Float-fishing methods on the heavily-fished bream rivers of

H

Eastern England and parts of Somerset are very different to methods for fish residing in other waters. Bream are usually found towards the middle in these Fen rivers and there are lots of times when anglers have to cast very close to the far bank. This may involve distances of up to forty yards. These extreme distances are really too great for even the most suitable of float-fishing methods and it is in situations like this that legering has scored.

The further a float has to be cast the greater is the amount of weight required to get it there. At these extreme ranges the tackle is exposed to mounting problems affecting bait presentation. The greater the distance the more difficult it becomes to counteract surface drift. A bad wind makes accuracy of casting more difficult to achieve. The sum total of these various problems gradually tends to make float fishing less practical at extreme range.

Some floats will cast and behave better than others. It is not purely and simply a matter of sheer weight that allows anglers to cast long distances, but rather one of balance. The float must be designed so that it flights through the air without deviation from its course. Although I wouldn't, of course, claim to have worked hand in hand with modern aircraft designers, the fact remains that the floats I use bear some comparison to the shape of the bodies of present-day jet airliners. The problems of a float and an aeroplane are similar in that they have to combat the same sort of problems in flight.

The weight in a modern fast-flying aircraft is well forward and this same principle is observed in my floats for bream rivers. But just as aircraft are no longer made of steel, being made from lighter alloys, so the best casting floats are also made from light materials. Some men still use balsa and cane floats but it is beyond dispute that cork and peacock quill casts immeasurably better.

Of course, I do use balsa and cane in some circumstances, but these are basically when I fish for roach in flowing water. For other sorts of fishing I prefer my floats to have peacock-quill stems, and if they have bodies for these to be made from cork.

Peacock and cork combine to provide floats which are very light but buoyant enough to take plenty of shot for the necessary casting weight. Thus they are ideal for long casting in wide and/or deep still waters and those where the flow is slight. Another very important feature of these floats is that they cast very well under adverse conditions.

To obtain accurate and long-distance casting I use a different casting technique from most anglers. I prefer to let the rod do the work and not to rely on sheer weight to reach the distance. Many men cast direct to the water. This tends to exaggerate the surface impact—and won't do for me. I prefer to give the float a lot of air when casting.

The flight of the float through the air is on the howitzer principle. It curves through the air in a pronounced arc to end by dropping lightly on to the surface of the water. See Fig. 38. I give my rod a full circular swing and always cast overarm, except when fishing in situations where I am forced to cast underarm because of bank-side obstructions like bushes and vegetation.

Remember, the less strain there is in casting the more accurate it is likely to be. The key to successful fishing is to land the float and terminal tackle in exactly the same position at each cast. To deviate

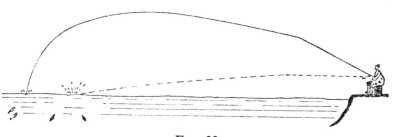

FIG. 38

Casting high into the air on the howitzer principle the float creates less surface impact than when it is cast directly at the water

from this means that catching fish is slowed down and this can be disastrous for the matchman.

We are in an era of the sliding float and I am just as keen on these floats as anyone else. I never believe in casting the full depth of the water with the float in a fixed position, when the depth is greater than six feet.

The advantages are obvious. Take a deep water, the Great Ouse Relief Channel, for instance. The depth there is up to sixteen feet. No man can successfully cast with his float fixed at that depth, for he would never achieve either accuracy or distance with his casting. Obviously, the Relief Channel is an extreme example, for there are not many waters as deep as that one, but it does illustrate the principle. And it applies equally as well to shallower waters where long casting is necessary.

The great advantage with sliding floats is that when the cast is being made all the weight—except for two tiny terminal shot—is in one compact heap. It is easier to cast a weight of one ounce than two weights of half an ounce each, particularly when—with fixed float fishing—the two weights are as much as ten feet apart.

With the weight in one compact heap—shot and float together—accuracy comes easily enough. But casting should never be strained. If you are using a float that carries only enough weight to reach the required position with exertion, then there is every reason to change to a float that carries more shot. Never overdo shotting weight but, at the same time, it is even more futile to try to persevere with less shot than you really need.

Many anglers get into a complete muddle trying to find the exact depth when preparing to fish with a sliding float. They are often feet, never mind inches, out and this doesn't give them much chance when they start to fish.

I have a fool-proof of finding the depth but it takes time. The depth cannot be accurately gauged with a single cast and casting must be repeated until the depth has been gauged to the inch. As I have already said, my shotting for a sliding float takes the form of a bunch of main shot at the lower limit of the fall of the float and then two other small shot down the line. I leave out one of those uppermost swan shot and replace it with two AAA—exactly the same weight but two shot instead of one.

I place one AAA where the swan shot would have been—with the other heavy shot—and place the remaining AAA just below the lower of the small shot. This will then be about fifteen inches from the hook. I would place the whole swan shot in that lower position but for the fact that if I did I wouldn't be able to cast far enough to reach the position I intend to fish. Such a big shot in that lower position hampers casting.

I know even before I make the first cast exactly how the float will set in the water when it is taking the full weight of all the shot. I roughly estimate the depth and cast to the position I shall fish.

If I haven't set the float deep enough the float takes the full weight of all the shot and I see the tip peeping above the surface. I reel in and move the stop knot a foot. On casting again, if the float is still not set deep enough, the same thing happens. Exactly the same amount of float shows above the surface. So I reel in again and add more depth. This time I may be over-depth. Instead of the float showing fractionally above the surface, the weight of that bottom AAA shot doesn't register on the float since it will be lying on the bottom. Therefore between one and a half and two inches of the tip of the float will protrude above the surface.

Now to find the exact depth. It lies somewhere between the present depth at which the float is set and the depth at which it was set for

hat previous cast. So I half the distance between the two and cast
gain.

By casting and adjusting an inch at a time I eventually establish
he lowest point at which the smallest amount of float shows above
he water. When I have done that I have the correct depth. I now
emove that bottom AAA shot and also the one added to the main
hot. I then replace their total weight with the swan shot. I am ready
o begin fishing, knowing exactly how much of my hook length is
ying on the bottom. I prefer to start fishing for bream with my bait
aid on the bottom in this way. See Fig. 39.

My standard sliding-float rig for bream is designed to catch fish
hat are down on, or very close to, the bottom. In the summer,
articularly in the deeper slower-moving bream waters, the fish often

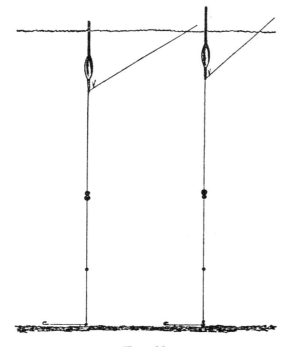

FIG. 39

The right and wrong ways of assessing the depth when
using a sliding float. When a big shot is placed close to
the lower of the small shot much more of the float tip
protrudes above the surface, giving a better visual
indication when the lower shot are on the bottom

rise off the bottom and feed in mid-water. This happens much mor
in the summer than in the winter, but even though fish may have bee.
down on the bottom when fishing began they do sometimes swir
higher up in the water to feed on groundbait falling towards them.

As the groundbait floats down to them they rise off the bottom t
get to it before it falls to ground. When they rise in this way bait
fished on the bottom are unlikely to be very successful.

Over recent years I have been practising with a method which I ar
sure will deal most capably with mid-water fish—whether they ar
roach or bream. This is to fish with a sliding float and to fish on th
drop at the same time. At first sight this might seem a very difficu'
proposition but it is really quite simple. The first requirement is
special range of floats taking from three AAA to two and a ha'
swan shot (five AAA). My float is a cork-bodied peacock quill wit
a very thin inset into the upper half of the stem. This inset is also c
peacock quill.

To explain the functions of the float let's assume I am using th
float taking two and a half swan shot. The two swan shot will set th
float to the mark where the thin inset begins and the remaining shc
sets the tip. If the depth is sixteen feet I set the float so that it casts
depth of eight feet and slides the other eight feet. The float slides o
a base ring only and is stopped at sixteen feet by a nylon stop kno

The two swan shot are placed together eight feet from the hool
acting as the lower stop for the float. This leaves the half swan shc
—an AAA—still to be positioned. It is of vital importance that ther
should only be one shot below the swan shot— two will defeat th
whole purpose of the tackle. For the bites all show when the floa
fails to set after the proper amount of time has been allowed for th
lower shot to drop that remaining eight feet.

I appreciate that an AAA may be too much weight to have dow
below and that sometimes one BB shot is enough. If this is the cas
then the other BB—two BB shot equal one AAA—is nipped on wit
the swan shot. But it is important that the lower shot should b
capable of moving a sizeable proportion of that thin inset in the tc
of the float or bites will be difficult to spot. And it is equally impor
ant that the lower shot should be quite close to the hook itse'
I consider twelve inches none too close.

When the tackle is cast out the compact weight of the swan sho
quickly sets the float to the bottom of the inset. See Fig. 40. At th
stage the float has settled back on to the nylon stop and the swar
are eight feet down. But that lower shot is still sinking and when th
float first sets the shot will be higher in the water than the swan shot.

Now comes the time when bites may be expected. The rate of fa of the bait is very much slower under the weight of the one small bottom shot than it was under the compact bunch. But it will take a specific period of time after the float first sets before the weight of the lower shot registers on the float, sinking it to its lower limit. See Fig. 41. It is during this period when the bait is falling that lower distance that the fish will take it. When a fish does grab the bait it inevitably delays the fall of the shot. Thus the fish, instead of the float, takes the weight of the lower shot and the float fails to settle as expected. See Fig. 42.

It is vital to know just how long is needed before that lower shot gets down. Once this is known, then each time the float remains high in the water at the end of the falling period, this must be a bite. All you have to do is strike. There's no need to look for any other sort of bite indication. The fact that more of the float is showing than should be is your bite indication.

You will see from this why it is necessary to have only one shot below the main bunch. If there were two the float would settle in three stages instead of two, and the uppermost part of the tip would move a shorter distance each time. If the surface is choppy it is best to have that float settling two inches in one movement rather than an inch each time. Thus you can clearly see when the float has failed to set itself correctly.

It is necessary to strike a fine balance between the thickness of the tip of the float for visibility's sake and its length. Obviously the thicker the upper half of the float, the less distance it will move when taking the weight of the bottom shot. But, at the same time, if it is too thin then you will find difficulty in seeing it at all, particularly in a water like the Relief Channel where, odds are, you will be fishing a long way out.

The rule is to use a thicker stem for really long casting but when fishing this method under the rod top—as I frequently do on the River Weaver for roach—then the tip can be very fine. The method can, of course, be used in a great many of our slower-moving rivers and drains, but to get the best out of it then groundbaiting must be to such a style that the fish are kept in their off-the-bottom position.

It is pointless carrying on fishing on the drop when the fish have settled back on the bottom, so I use a slow-sinking groundbait, and squatts are the ideal maggot feed. I have always found it pays to throw in two balls of groundbait in fairly rapid succession. One ball brings the fish up and the second tends to keep them up. If only a single ball is used then the fish tend to follow it down to the bottom.

This method is particularly worthwhile if the water temperature is high. The fish are then more likely to be in mid-water or thereabouts

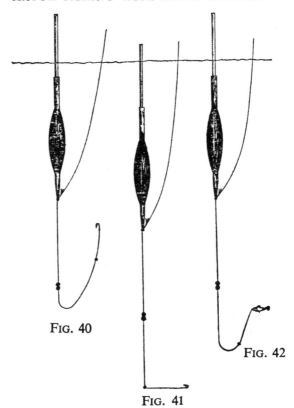

FIG. 40

FIG. 42

FIG. 41

Taking fish 'on the drop' with the sliding float. Fig.
40 shows the float taking the weight of the main
bunch of shot but with one shot still falling and yet to
register on the float. When this shot has fallen its full
distance it will set the float as in Fig. 41. But if
sufficient time has been allowed for the bottom shot to
have fallen into position and the float remains high in
the water then a fish must have taken the bait and is
also holding the weight of the bottom shot as in
Fig. 42

of their own accord. And that is where they prefer to feed—if you
give them the chance.

Now let's look at another method of catching fish that are feeding
on the bed of the river. This is a method particularly suited to the
deeper waters. It is of great importance that this method should only

be used when the water is dead still. If there is any flow at all, then
the rig is defeated.

It is a method of float legering and calls for a nylon stop on the
line. The float must be quite buoyant—but not too buoyant. It must
be capable of being held in the fishing position by a $\frac{1}{4}$ oz. Arlesey
bomb.

I again favour a cork-bodied peacock quill, for peacock has natural
buoyancy and will hold up to the surface very much better than cane.
The slider is again fastened to the base ring only. It is a compact
float about four inches long, with a body two inches long and seven-
eighths inch at its widest point and tapered to each end. The leger is
allowed to slide between two split shot three feet six inches apart.
The distance between the baited hook and the bottom stop shot
should be short. A few inches is often enough.

The exact position of the nylon stop checking the upward movement of the float can only be found by trial and error, but it depends
on the depth of the water and the distance one is casting. For a reasonable cast of twenty-five yards on the Relief Channel something close
to thirty feet from the hook is about right. As a useful guide, I have
found that the nylon stop should always be set at approximately
double the depth of the water you are fishing.

The cast is made. As soon as the lead hits the bottom the rod top
is thrust about three inches below the surface, the surplus line reeled
in and the line sunk. The line is kept taut.

The natural buoyance of the float sends it bobbing up the line
until it is held by the nylon stop. Ideally, with the rod top retained
below the surface those three inches, the float should peep above the
surface at the nylon stop. The accurate setting of the float is arrived
at by winding in slowly with the reel handle until the float peeps
above the surface. See Fig. 43.

Each cast must be a near-identical distance. A difference of a foot
or two can be made good by the way you hold the rod, but when the

FIG. 43

A delicate method of taking bream that are feeding on
the bottom in a deep still-water drain or lake

difference runs to yards then the nylon stop will have to be moved if the method is to be effective.

In the case of this float-legering method the bite shows in a very marked fashion. As the fish takes the bait it moves the small bomb which is already offsetting the buoyancy of the float. As the bream moves the bomb the float lifts sharply into the air. Strike and the fish should be yours.

This method works best on sizeable bream; fish of $1\frac{1}{2}$ lb. upwards. But it needs an even bottom. If the bed is uneven then the bomb can foul either on a stone or on an obstruction. The bite may not register on the float at all. This is not a sure-fire method. Fishing conditions have to be perfect or it is a waste of time, but on the days when it does work it will bring some very heavy bags of bream.

I remember one occasion when I was fishing the Ten Mile Bank stretch of the Great Ouse. The water was still but I couldn't hook many fish on my normal sliding float rig, despite being 'shelled' (the maggot being stripped) many times. Switching to this rig I have just described, I took bream after bream and finished with a catch that must have weighed 70 lb. But remember, this method is only completely effective when used against biggish bream.

Although the line is kept tight, imposing a direct pull on the small bomb—thus nullifying most of the bomb's holding power on the bottom—small bream will not always pull at the bait sufficiently strongly to cause the bomb to move. Some bites show as the float sinks when the fish move further out into the water, drawing line through the Arlesey bomb's ring. But many bites will be from fish that are moving in towards the bank. These must actually move the bomb for the bites to show as lifts. The float rises up and sometimes even topples over. These bites are usually from bigger fish.

Anglers fishing waters where there is a mixed stock of fish should always give some thought to the weight of fish they are likely to need in order to win a match. This cannot be assessed with complete accuracy but at least a target can be set. And it is the progress made towards that target that dictates very largely how each man will fish.

If he falls badly behind schedule the stage arrives when, if he has been fishing for small bream, for example, he no longer has sufficient fishing time remaining to reach his target. Therefore, he has no alternative but to change over to fishing for bigger bream. He may not get them, but at least it is worth trying, for otherwise whatever he catches will not get him into the prize list. This assessment, of course, is for individual fishing only. In a team contest each man cannot set himself a target since he does not know what his colleagues' efforts will be. He just has to carry on fishing, taking th highest weight his swim can possibly produce.

Only the most rash of anglers will ignore bream when fishing big open contests. There was a time in 1965 when Northwich anglers had a fine run of team weights made up with roach taken under the rod top. They even won a number of individual firsts but success with this method did not last. Disease affected the roach in some rivers. This and the failure of the roach to feed in others made this style unprofitable after 1965.

It is, however, a well-known fact that big roach on many rivers will feed close to one bank or the other. These were the fish the Northwich anglers fished for, but their method had severe limitations and I would never fish that style myself.

I want the best of both worlds. I want to know whether roach or bream are present in my swim in the biggest quantity and then to fish for the species that gives me the best chance of a good weight. There are times when I have to go for both species and, when I do, I have never found any difficulty in getting small bream to take casters.

The great blessing of casters is that in most rivers the swim does not have to be fed heavily to keep the fish interested. A dozen or so thrown in at a time is ample and two pints are sufficient for most contests. Further, the casters are thrown in loose. This means there is no cereal feed to fill them up and the fish are therefore ready for the hookbait.

At first I thought that this new rod-end style for roach could revolutionise match fishing. I thought it was being done on casters. But it wasn't. The hookbait was an anattoed gozzer—a colour-fed 'special' maggot. When there were a number of men going for roach and they were pegged close together it has been noticeable they didn't do so well. They had to share the fish, and there were not enough to give each man enough for a place in the prize list.

I don't really care for the idea of playing fish where I have hooked them. That's why I prefer to hook mine further out in the river. There's much less disturbance of the important part of the swim— where the fish are being hooked. The Northwich style was to avoid catching fish on the drop. They couldn't avoid them altogether but their aim was to get the bait down quickly to the big roach.

They feed their swims heavily with something like a gallon of squatts and fourteen pounds of groundbait. Loose feeding with squatts is not enough. The feed has to sink quite quickly to keep the fish near the bottom.

To avoid the smaller fish these roach anglers do not cast in the usual way. When they put the bait into the water it is a 'drop in' in the strict sense.

The shot enters the water first and sinks before the float touches the water. Thus the bait sinks quickly, giving the small fish little time to take it before it reaches bottom. But in a 12 lb. catch of roach made this way there will be an average of 6 lb. of small roach and 6 lb. of better fish weighing from 8 oz. to anything up to 2 lb.

A number of fish are lost, for the anglers use very small hooks—sometimes as tiny as size 22. Shotting is by two small shot to a tiny length of peacock quill.

I like to catch roach when I can. I would never fish in a way that eliminated all chances of catching them unless I was absolutely certain of other species. But neither would I fish in a style that gave me no chances of catching bream. Bream are the fish that win most big matches and, even if I could have a reasonable chance of taking 12 lb. of roach, I couldn't accept that as the limit of my swim. There might be some big bream, or quantities of smaller ones, out in the middle of the river. No matchman can seriously afford to ignore this possibility as a matter of habit.

Match fishing in still-water lakes calls for long casting. When a man fishes on his own there may be no need whatsoever to cast much further than the end of his rod, but when large numbers of men are fishing quite close together it is almost impossible to catch any number of fish close inshore. I have a very wide experience of fishing such places and can claim a remarkable record at Welbeck Lakes. I have won seven of the nineteen matches I have fished there and been placed in the top ten in the remainder. The lowest number of anglers fishing in any of these contests was 300 and the maximum 500. I have never yet fished in the small lake without taking the top catch from that particular water.

I have always made it my policy to fish no less than fifteen yards out and, at times, have fished as much as twenty-five yards away from the bank. The earlier wins came using maggots but as casters began to prove so deadly I used them at Welbeck with success.

The first occasion when I took casters to Welbeck I didn't have the confidence to use them. So I fished with maggots—and won. But at the end of the match, instead of packing up, I moved to a swim in the little lake. It had been fished in the contest and very little had been caught there. I fished for an hour and a half and in that time caught 7 lb. to 8 lb. of roach. The astonishing fact about that catch was that many of the fish were on the 7 oz. mark—in a water where the best roach taken on maggot weighed no more than 5 oz. and the average was very much less. In the match I had just won with maggots my best fish had weighed only 4 oz.

I used to use a stick float taking three BB shot and could cast the

:quired distance comfortably. But other anglers were getting wise.
hey too started fishing further out and I was driven to casting
urther myself. The match rules allowed me to use both a catapult
nd a throwing stick and this undoubtedly helped me to catch big
eights of fish. I didn't often have to use groundbait and could get
1y caster feed exactly where I wanted it.

But as I had to cast further and further out I eventually fished
eyond the range it was possible to feed with the throwing stick and
ad to use the catapult all the time. In the course of these matches
hich lasted between three and five hours, I used a maximum of two
ints of casters. On occasions when there was an adverse wind I was
>rced to use small balls of groundbait as a means of getting the
1sters far enough out, but my results have continued to be good.

The same basic technique was used in Rudyard Lake, my favourite
ater. But Rudyard, unlike Welbeck, contains large numbers of
ream. It has, in fact, proved a great blessing, and during the spell
hen roach were feeding badly in all my local waters—and on
udyard too—I could go there and get a good catch of bream. In
ict, this water continues to increase in popularity each year as more
nd more anglers fish it.

When Fenland matches began to be won with leger methods, I
sed to travel to Rudyard very regularly. There are no bream in Fir
ree flash and I had to practise on bream since they were the fish I
ould have to catch in the Fens. I fished mainly with a butt-bite
idicator and this taught me how to feed for bream and how to
itch them on the bottom and on the drop. I learned, once I had
erfected the method, that I could catch bream quicker with a bite
idicator than with a float. I have had many mixed catches, all sizes
f bream up to 3 lb. 11 oz. and many roach to 12 oz. The best
ggregate catch touched 40 lb. and many exceeded 20 lb.

One factor, often overlooked, is that on big still-water lakes the
ind causes a circulating movement of the water. There is a pro-
>unced flow in the opposite direction to the wind along the banks.
his makes it ideal for fishing, since the feed is carried along with
1e flow and this is a factor which undoubtedly helps to bring the
sh into the swim. But if they fail to take this into account anglers
ho fish with a leger can so easily place their baits clear of the patch
1ey have groundbaited.

Index

Printed in Great Britain by The Anchor Press Ltd., Tiptree, Essex